Thoughts on

SMALL BOAT RACING

Rosenfeld

There is seldom time for any detailed analysis in a tight situation.

Thoughts on

SMALL BOAT RACING

by

C. STANLEY OGILVY

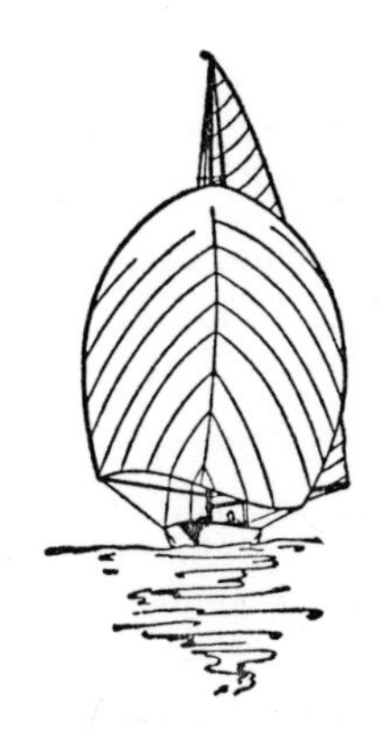

D. VAN NOSTRAND COMPANY, INC.

PRINCETON, NEW JERSEY

TORONTO LONDON

NEW YORK

EDITED AND DESIGNED BY EUGENE V. CONNETT

FIRST EDITION

PRINTED IN THE UNITED STATES OF AMERICA

Published simultaneously in Canada by
D. VAN NOSTRAND COMPANY (Canada), LTD.

Library of Congress Catalog Card No. 57-11310

D. VAN NOSTRAND COMPANY, INC.

120 Alexander St., Princeton, New Jersey
257 Fourth Avenue, New York 10, New York
25 Hollinger Rd., Toronto 16, Canada

All correspondence should be addressed to the principal office of the company at Princeton, N. J.

Acknowledgment

Parts of two chapters contain material previously published as articles in *Yachting* magazine; and part of Chapter 13 was included in a section on sails written for "Encyclopedie du Yachting—La Plaisance," Kister, Geneva, under direction of Louis Doliveux. The permission of both editors to include these items in the present book is gratefully acknowledged.

Contents

1	The Skipper Who Wins	1
2	Know Your Boat	5
3	Expecting the Unexpected	15
4	Starting Tactics	28
5	To Windward in Unsteady Breezes	42
6	Sail Your Own Race	52
7	Series Strategy	64
8	Crewing	71
9	Tides	81
10	The Weather	89
11	The Rules	101
12	NAYRU and IYRU	112
13	Sails	124
14	The Purpose of It All	137
15	Afterthought	142
	Index	145

List of Illustrations

There is seldom time for any detailed analysis in a tight situation. *Frontispiece*

K-5 squeezes past the anchor line of the committee boat for the best start. 20

No. 3130 gets away on the port tack into undisturbed air. 21

The wind goes dead around a starting area. 52

"A mammoth puff dismasted *Flower*." 53

Current revealed by a buoy. 84

"Unable or unwilling to jibe." 85

A radially cut jib. 116

A mainsail with two windows. 117

CHAPTER 1

The Skipper Who Wins

Why are there so few books about yacht racing? Other games have hundreds of them. Books on how to play better tennis, how to improve your golf, how to do almost anything, appear by the dozen every year; but there are not many books on how to win more sailboat races—so few that most eager skippers have read them all. You couldn't begin to cover the field so easily in most popular sports. Why is the racing library so meager? One answer might be that sailing is not as "popular" as something like golf or tennis. It does not have so many participants. This may be true, but I do not believe it is the whole answer. Sailing is growing in popularity every year as an ever increasing proportion of the population somehow finds its way into boats. But even if small boat racing were to become as universal as any game you could name, I doubt if there would ever be many books about it. The sport simply doesn't lend itself to "how to do" literature. Why are there no books by great violinists on how to become a violin virtuoso? Just ask any violin player. "Don't be silly," he'll answer. "In order to become a violinist you don't read books; you go and practice on the instrument."

This is close to the answer to how to win more races: go and practice on the instrument. Go out and sail more races, and after a while you will begin to win some of them. This should be the philosophy behind any yacht racing book. A book can help only a little: it can guide the way, perhaps organize your thoughts and start you working and thinking in the direction which will ultimately lead to more successful results on the water. Sailing is an art, like playing the violin, and there is only one way to get better at it, and that is by practice.

But sailboat *racing* is a competitive sport as well as an art (and perhaps partially a science too). And it is in the various aspects of racing that hints and suggestions can most readily be given and received. This is a book strictly about racing—and highly competitive racing. It presupposes that you are out there on the course for just one reason: to win. Oh, there may be other reasons, to be sure, like escaping from your mother-in-law; but you could have done that just as well by day-sailing. As soon as you start to *race,* your principle concern must be to get across that finish line first or as near to first as you possibly can. This is the thrill that you seek, the reward of all your efforts. Unless you are interested in winning, this book is not for you.

The factors that go into the successful campaigning of a small sailboat can be roughly cataloged under two main headings: (1) the technique of making the boat go faster through the water; and (2) all other considerations. Under (1) there is much to be said about conditioning the hull and rig, tuning, trim, arrangement of hardware and fittings, spars, sails and all other gear, and most important of all, helmsmanship—the art of steering the boat. Except incidentally and by way of illustration, you will find little about any of these things in this book. They are the subject of an earlier book,* and have been ably handled in some of the other texts to which you will find references from time to time in the footnotes. A major exception is the sail chapter; and the excuse for that is that the invention of the synthetic materials has changed sails and sailmaking so drastically that practically everything five years old is out of date. That was what determined me to take up this topic; and the discussion of cutting, material, draft, balance, and all the rest

* The author's *Successful Yacht Racing,* W. W. Norton & Co., Inc., (1951.)

of it is so closely linked with trim and sail handling that technical details could not be avoided.

You may have been wondering what is left for item No. 2, "all other considerations." I suggest a glance at the chapter headings, in the table of contents. All the factors listed there are vitally important in winning races, just as important as making the boat go fast. Variations on this theme appear again and again throughout the book, which might indeed have been called "It's the skipper who wins, not the boat."

It usually happens that the best way to illustrate a point is to draw on personal experience. I must apologize for the frequent references to races in which I have sailed. This is not a technique which I like; yet these are the races I know about, and there seems no way of disguising the fact that I am the principal character involved. The contract bridge expert has a great advantage in writing his books. He can modestly say, "South, whose partner's over-enthusiasm had landed the contract in six spades, was able by astute deduction to develop the only possible line of play which could make the bid." Only the most naive reader fails to discern that South was in fact the author. In writing this book I have no such shield to hide behind. I am dreadfully embarrassed by the fact that in most of the incidents described, our hero of the first person singular comes out ahead. The predicament seems unavoidable: these are the incidents that made the greatest impression on me at the time, and consequently they are the ones that I remember. Let me assure you that over the years I have done badly many, many more times than I have done well in races; and I am sure that anyone else who has kept an honest count must come to the same conclusion.

Another apology must be made for the too frequent references to Stars. I have owned one of these boats for more than twenty years; and although some of my racing has been done in other classes, the majority of it has been in Stars. For this reason also I have become accustomed to referring to "the crew" when I mean only one person forward. "Crewman" seems an awkward word, and the use of the word crew in the singular sense causes no real difficulty. It is hoped that you will find that everything in the book can be applied equally to any boat, keel or centerboard, with any number of people in crew.

But enough of explanatory notes: let's get on with the business at hand.

CHAPTER 2

Know Your Boat

The other day a squall hit our harbor. It was an ordinary summer squall, not very severe; you could see it coming minutes ahead. Just outside the harbor two small boats were being sailed by club Juniors. They were in no serious trouble: one boat lowered its jib, the other chose to lower its mainsail, and both were weathering the squall adequately. But were they left to their own devices? They were not. A launch with the yacht club manager himself aboard to intensify the sense of crisis must needs go to their "rescue" and tow them in. By the time they had reached the float the storm was spent and it was already flat calm.

I chanced to be watching these procedures from a yacht moored in the harbor. During the storm there was another tiny white sail outside, apparently overlooked by the shepherding launch. After the storm I rowed out to see how the little catboat had fared. It was manned by a single youngster who, as I arrived, was shaking out a reef. (How many Junior *instructors,* let alone their charges, know how to tie in a reef?) "Have any trouble?" I asked. " 'Course not—just got wet," was the cheery answer. "So long!" And he hoisted his sail—and sat there, since there was now no wind. Disturbed about not getting a tow to his harbor, a couple of miles down the coast? Not at all. Later, the wind would come up, maybe. Meanwhile he would dry out in the sun and bail out the boat and watch the angry clouds tumbling and rumbling away to the east. And there was always the paddle . . .

Who learned more about their boats that day, the carefully instructed Juniors or the solo pilot in the catboat?

To become thoroughly acquainted with a boat is not as simple as you may think. The process has far-reaching implications. How long will it take to get to know your boat? You might as well ask how long it will take to get to know your wife. Maybe five years, maybe a lifetime. I have owned and raced one boat for the past ten years, and have put so much time and thought and effort into the old bucket that I am loathe to get a new one. When most of your summertime existence for ten years has centered around one boat, you hate to part with it. Why, the *Flame* and I are just getting to know each other!

It is my conviction that ultimate success with a small racing boat implies personal maintenance. The skippers who get the best results usually do most of their own work. My boat has been back to the shop only once since it was built, and that was because a major repair job had to be done on a bottom plank. Except for that, it has never been touched by a professional carpenter or painter.

I have nothing against boat yards and professional painters. In fact I am perfectly willing to admit that some yards (only a few) could do a better job on my boat than I do. But the psychology is all wrong. If you do your own work you care for your boat like a baby. You are in no hurry to dent the topside or scratch the bottom paint when you know that to do so means hours of painstaking repair work. Small boats today get towed all over the country on trailers, which is admittedly very hard on them. The chances of marring the paint job are greatly increased by trailing. There is a growing tendency among racing skippers to let the boat run down toward the end of the season; the rail is full of dents, the bottom is pitted with road tar and gravel bruises, and the deck is scratched and dirty. The owner apologizes for the boat's appearance, and says "She's going back to the builder's for a complete overhaul and refinish this winter, so what's another dent or two?" Such an owner soon finds that this becomes an annual (and expensive) habit. But it's not the expense that I object to, it's the frame of mind. The skipper who has a yard do the maintenance usually does so on the grounds that he hasn't the time to do his own work. This is the same skipper who can't find the time to sail the boat very often between races; nor does he have time to go aboard early on race day to putter about a bit before making sail. He may not realize it, but this fellow whose time is so valuable doesn't have time to win many races.

Taking care of the boat is part of getting in the mood for sailing. While you work on the boat you think about things nautical, and your mind works, almost subconsciously and quite painlessly, on some problem of racing. While you are repairing something, the chances are that you will be reminded of something else that ought to be done. Certainly there is no end to the improvements that can be made on even a small boat. You just won't think of these things if you have someone else do all the work.

In this mechanized world there is a lamentable falling off in the ability of the individual to minister to his own needs. Today we seldom have the skills required to repair or re-build the complicated devices on which our creature comforts depend. We send for the service man, and as often as not he in turn sends for a new unit from the factory. Everything is factory made, nothing hand turned. Craftsmanship has gone out of fashion.

There is pride in owning something that *you* have made beautiful with your own hands. There is also a sort of sympathetic rapport which gradually builds up between you and a boat you know well. You somehow feel, after a few years, that you at last understand the boat and the boat understands you. This is sheer fantasy, of course; but there is no fantasy in the fact that you work more smoothly and efficiently and with less conscious effort—and this is translated into winning more races —with a boat every inch of which you are thoroughly familiar with.

Working on a racing boat is not drudgery. Many people think that preparing the bottom for painting is perhaps the year's worst job. I do not find it so. Some weekend next spring, when the sun is shining, I shall wheel the boat out of its shelter and turn it on its side, as I have done every spring for years, and go to work with wet sandpaper. As I get my back into it and the surface turns smooth as glass under the sanding block, all the kinks and mental stresses of the winter will begin to relax, and as one by one I pick up the threads of the racing world where they were so rudely broken off last fall I shall dream and scheme of the fine contests to come. Each stroke of the sandpaper represents a smoother, faster bottom, and I shall spare no effort, though I might acquire a stiff muscle or two the first day . . . This is drudgery? I am looking forward to it already.

The human mind works in devious and wonderful ways. Many thought processes are only half conscious. If you think about a problem, and turn it over and mull it about a bit in your mind, the solution often pops up almost by itself. If small boat racing is a big enough part of your life and thought, your mind cannot avoid becoming correspondingly well stocked with racing material. Many problems will be solved before they arise. Decisions in moments of crisis will come easily to you because the necessary information will all be there, neatly stored away ready to be called upon.

I have long suspected that just thinking about sailing—which is another way of saying training your mind in this direction—makes one a better sailor. Recently there have appeared many scientific writings confirming this theory. To quote just one: "The circuits of the mind improve vastly with use and exercise. Thinking in a given way brings an increased blood supply and more nourishment to the cells and synapses involved. The process we call learning consists of setting up mental switching patterns over and over again, to train certain circuits and groups of switchboards to function together. The mind needs to be exercised and disciplined as well as to have its gates thrown open through interest." *

Alfred Stanford has explored this idea very thoroughly as it applies specifically to boats and boating in THE PLEASURES OF SAILING, (Simon & Schuster, 1943). The whole book can be read with profit. He says: "When my boat is hauled out, I find myself spending hours just walking around her, looking at this loose spot of bottom paint to see if underneath there is a fastening bung missing. I like to see with my own eyes that when she is painted, the back of the rudder stock gets a good dose of anti-fouling paint in an area usually skipped. I like to make sure that the strainers are really removed from the engine water intake and the usual cluster of obstructing barnacles scraped away. Aside from these specific objectives, I also just like to walk around her and dream.

"I keep getting new understanding of her lines every time I study her so. This must mean that a lot of subtle things register too. The basis for a feeling of intimacy is laid. A kinship with the whole boat grows. Perhaps it is only a feeling. But the part of my boat I seldom see, I do see when she is on the slipway. I know what is there, under me, when later she is afloat, and I know that it is good and sound."

All this mooning about and brooding over the boat pays off in direct as well as indirect ways. For one thing, you notice things that would otherwise escape detection. Who are the people who have the "bad luck" to break down? Usually those who rush down to the boat on race day, hurry aboard, and make the starting line just in time for the gun. How can they possibly

* "How the Brain Works," by George R. Harrison, *The Atlantic Monthly*, September, 1956.

know the condition of all the multitudinous components of the rig? Sometimes, to be sure, rigging will fail despite the most meticulous inspection. But very often weaknesses can be detected and checked. Many times I have come across evidences of fatigue in hardware or fittings, or a telltale broken strand of wire has sent me hustling to the rigger. You don't see these little signs if you don't look around. Last summer during a routine inspection I came to a single tiny wire strand sticking out of a piece of 7×19 wire. Now one strand of 7×19 wire is only one part in 133 that make up the cable. Why not let it go? Certainly 132/133 of the wire is strong enough! This philosophy only courts disaster. On closer examination I found to my great surprise that the whole 19-strand core was broken. It would not have been long before the rest went with it.

On the other hand, what is likely to happen if you are in too great a hurry? Some years ago we had trailed the boat to the Great South Bay (Long Island) Race Week; and because the launching facilities were farther from the race course than we had anticipated, we rigged and launched in a great flurry and set out at once for the starting line. We made it, and started the race in a typical Bay southwester, which is a good brisk breeze. I was just on the point of going about onto the port tack when I happened to glance to leeward and saw to my horror the port main lower shroud dangling in the water six or eight feet to leeward of the hull, attached only at its upper end! Somebody (I have to admit it was I) had failed to open the cotter in the clevis pin fastening the shroud to the turnbuckle, and the whole thing had come adrift. Tacking without a lower shroud would probably have meant the loss of the mast in that chop. Fortunately we were able to stay on the starboard tack long enough to make frenzied repairs. . . . A very close call indeed.

What else can you do with your boat, besides care for it and admire it and dream about it? Well, you can sail it. Sail it every chance you get: to and from races, evenings during the week, weekends in the spring before the racing season starts. You may not be able to point to any one specific new skill that you acquire each time you go out; but like the boy in the catboat, every single hour of sailing makes you a better sailor. It certainly makes you one hour better acquainted with your boat and—what is more important—your boat's performance in the water.

Tight situations develop in every race calling for split second decisions which depend upon accurate knowledge of exactly what the boat will do and how it will respond. You never have time to analyze the situation in detail at the time. Your course of action must be based not on a carefully reasoned decision with all the factors weighed and the odds precisely calculated; rather it must be based on knowledge and judgment drawn from experience. You choose Course *A* because it flashes at you out of your memory that Course *A* once worked before in a similar crisis; or Course *B* because you know, without asking yourself, that the boat will fetch that far and you will get away with it with a few feet to spare; or Course *C* because you tried the maneuver the other night in a practice sail and it seemed sound. The point is that if you do not have the necessary hours of sailing experience behind you to make the choice instantly, you may well find yourself taking Course *D,* the only one left because you waited too long to do any of the other things. Usually Course *D* is the one that fouls you out. Experienced skippers foul out of races too, but probably less frequently than inexperienced ones. One reason is that they do not take hair-raising chances so often. Another is that if forced to take a chance, they are better equipped to extricate themselves from the resulting jam without a catastrophe.

Consider the following situation which arises in almost every race. You cross the starting line on the starboard tack, along with everyone else, and sooner or later you want to go about.

You glance over your right shoulder, and of course there is a boat on your starboard quarter a few lengths astern and almost as far out abeam. Can you tack and cross the other boat? If you tack and can't make it, it will be too late then to bear off under her stern: you will instead be forced to tack back to starboard again for a costly loss.

I confess that after half a lifetime of small boat racing I am still not nearly as good as I want to be in answering this question. So very much depends on wind and sea conditions! In a good breeze with no sea you can point incredibly high, and furthermore you give away almost nothing in going about if you do it smartly. Under these conditions your competitor can be menacingly close and you can cross him easily. Even if at first it looks as though you cannot, you should at least go about and take another look from the new tack, because on this sort of day you can always sneak back to the starboard tack again, with your tail between your legs, without losing much. On the other hand, in a seaway your boat may come down hard on a wave in the middle of the tack and stop dead, something which in your optimism you hadn't counted on. The boat you thought yourself clear ahead of will be upon you by the time you gather way—and a nasty foul is imminent. Lots of sailing in company with another boat of the same class, practicing this maneuver many times and noting the results, in the cool of a pleasant evening without the tensions of the race to contend with, will go a long way toward making you an expert in solving the situation.

Here is another question on which I feel that not enough practical research has been done. There are two ways to put a small sloop about. One, which I think is favored by the majority of skippers, is to keep the jib full and drawing until the last possible moment, not slacking the old sheet until the boat is almost head to wind. Good crews pride themselves on being able to go from one sheet to the other with hardly a flutter of the sail in between. I am by no means convinced that this is the best procedure. It takes its support from the theory that while the bow is turning into the wind the jib will stay full much longer than the main, so why not utilize the drive thus available? The counter-theory is this: you don't get something for nothing. If you keep the jib filled while the boat is turning from full and by to head-to-wind, the jib is working *against the rudder* during that period, and consequently a boat that is put about in this fashion requires correspondingly more helm —a braking action that slows her down. It may be that this braking action is exactly counterbalanced by the increased drive obtained from the non-flapping jib; it is also possible that what is right for one type of boat is wrong for another. But I don't know, and I should certainly like to know. One way to find out would be to try it many times by one method, sailing alongside a friend who would go about together with you but by the other method. Then to cancel out any skill factor, reverse the roles of the two boats and run some more trials. Until I have a chance to make such a set of experiments, I'm letting my jib go the instant the helm *starts* to go down.

One more example: hardly anybody knows how to fill away correctly on a new tack. I arrive at this bald and uncomplimentary conclusion by observing jibsheet tenders who are accustomed to the ways of other helmsmen. I am not one of those fortunate individuals who has a steady crew. On the contrary, a wide variety of crews, more or less experienced, sail on the boat each summer. Most of them have had some training on other boats. Almost invariably they expect me to bear away below full and by for a few seconds after filling away on the new tack, "to gather good headway." On the *Flame* we have marks on the jibsheets, in the form of black threads sewn around the sheets at some location where they can conveniently be seen by the crew. Both sheets are marked exactly alike, so that once the position of the marks is established for the wind and the sea conditions which prevail, it is easy to trim the new sheet "to the mark" after going about. I generally forget to tell new crews that on this boat we trim to the marks immediately, with no nonsense about easing after each tack. Any easing of sheets means bearing off, which is equivalent to distance given away. If you are stopped so dead in the water after tacking that you have to reach to get going again then there is something the matter with the way you are tacking; and this goes for centerboarders as well as keel boats, except possibly in a really bad sea. The fact is that you should be able to point just slightly *higher* than normal before you gather full way, because of a freeing of the apparent wind.

But this is getting ahead of the story. We shall return to the apparent wind in a later chapter. Meanwhile we consider next a much neglected aspect of winning races.

CHAPTER 3

Expecting the Unexpected

If you have gained the impression from what has been said so far that all you have to do to win races is to want to win them—that you can dream your way into first place by wishful thinking—then let me hasten to disabuse you of this notion. Nobody has ever yet won a race by any kind of mental magic; it takes a lot of downright hard work, concentrated physical and mental effort. Dreamers who are not willing to work for the realization of their dreams may leave the room.

You must learn to take care of first things first. In sailing, this means acquiring an ability to notice and to act upon those factors and developments on which the outcome of the race depends. Most skippers become so absorbed in trying to make the boat go that they overlook matters of far greater importance. What, you may ask, could be more important than that? Well, several things.

There is no denying that sheer speed through the water is a necessity. It follows that it is essential to have the very best in sails and equipment, to get your boat properly tuned, and to keep her in top shape at all times. These are the ingredients of a championship boat. But they are only the *minimum* essentials for doing well in races. You can safely assume that all your best opponents will be about as well off as you are in this respect. What more can you do to best them?

The opinion seems to prevail in some quarters that the "hot" skippers have some carefully guarded secrets that help them win races. Usually these are assumed to be secrets of tuning. "If only I could get my boat tuned!" wails the novice. He thinks that if an expert would only come aboard his boat and take up one and a half turns on the right turnbuckle, the boat would immediately shift into high gear and start winning races. I am here to tell you that it doesn't work that way. Take for example the position of the mast. On Stars this is supposed to be a Big Deal. The first time we rigged the *Flame,* ten years ago, we threw the mast into what seemed a likely position in the step, (in a Star you have a range of about five inches either way from "neutral") and bolted down the vice. *We have never moved it* from that position. It wasn't just luck. I knew approximately where it should go from previous experience with Stars. But my point is that if it had happened to be an inch forward or aft of where it is, I am convinced that the boat would go just as well.

Under so-called ideal conditions, the speed, at which the skipper is able to sail the boat through the water is the only thing that counts. "Ideal conditions" mean to most people a dead beat to windward from a perfectly square line to a clearly visible first mark over an unobstructed course free of shoals and tides and clear of headlands in an absolutely steady breeze. Just how many such legs do you get each summer? And even that is only the beginning of the race. You may be first at the first mark of such a race and last at the finish. By all means have the boat in condition, so that it will go as fast as anyone else's and thus allow you to hold your own or better in the "ideal" races. But this is only a starter. What about all the other races, the crazy ones? Who "has all the luck" when things go haywire? Somehow this chap just happens to be in the right place at the right time, and he does it not only once but again and again. This skipper must be able to make his boat go, certainly; but he has learned how to come out on top in a host of other departments too.

This skipper is far from the dreamy type. Rather he is characterized by an intense alertness to what is going on around him. And now we come to a real secret weapon, if the novice must have one. Like most important procedures it is beautifully simple and can be practiced by anyone. It consists of two words: keep awake.

Don't get so wrapped up in sailing the boat in an attempt to gain three yards that you overlook a golden opportunity to gain three hundred. You think I am exaggerating? On the contrary I am if anything under-stating the case. *More races are won by alertness* than by superior speed.

For twenty years I have kept a log which runs now to eight volumes, recording briefly the story of every race sailed. Mostly this log is a story of my mistakes. To read it is very humbling: I certainly appear to be a terrible hacker, so many are the booboos recorded. One can be very objective in analyzing one's own sailing errors; it is easy to see afterwards what should have been done. Nearly always I should have been more alert; and whenever *Flame* or one of her predecessors did manage a win, it was hardly ever because she was moving through the water faster than anyone else, but almost always because, for a wonder, her skipper happened to make a vital observation in time. Let us look into some instances of the importance of alertness.

Racing skippers seem to operate under the basic assumption that the race committee is trying to run the race the way they, the racing skippers, would run it. After you get to know some race committees you will realize how far from the truth this is. Race committee members don't even think like skippers. The exception occurs when the really good skipper takes a day off to run the regatta. Then problems of the kind I am about to describe don't arise so often. But remember, the true racing men on race committees are about as rare as a beginner's trophies.

I have the greatest sympathy and respect for race committee men, and do not share the opinion common among skippers that all committee men should hang, except chairmen, who should be boiled in oil. The trouble with the skippers who hold this opinion is that they have never served on race committees. I heartily recommend such service to all racing men. It would open their eyes to some of the difficulties involved in committee work. I am not saying that it is impossible to run a perfect race; fortunately for our sanity, it often happens. I am simply pointing out that it isn't necessarily easy. And, because you are going to have to continue to race most of the time under committees who do make occasional mistakes, it behooves you to learn how to anticipate and even to exploit these mistakes.

Under North American Yacht Racing Union rule 40(b), the race committee may change the course at any time up to three minutes before the start. This is a beautiful illustration of a rule that was obviously written by committee men. It goes on to say that this should not be done if the change requires a shifting of sails "that cannot reasonably be completed within three minutes." I submit that the words in quotes are superfluous. In effect the sentence says that this should not be done if it requires a shifting of sails, period. I challenge any committee man, racing expert or no, to be notified *three minutes before his start* that he has to make an unexpected sail change, however simple; to make that change; and to get across the starting line on time. It just can't be done. The rule is, of course, a very poor one anyway: it nearly always causes confusion to change the course after the warning gun. By this time a skipper is so absorbed in trying to make a respectable start that he can't be expected to look again at the committee boat for a change in signals. It may, moreover, be physically impossible to see the signal board from the far end of the line; nor is three minutes sufficient time in which to sail over and have a look. The result is that half the skippers sail the old course, a great hullabaloo eventuates, and sometimes the race is disallowed. Sometimes, however, it stands; so whether we like it or not, it is up to skippers racing under these rules to glance at the signal board at the very last available opportunity, or to detail a member of the crew with binoculars to do so. Be alert to a possible change: expect the unexpected.

There exists an alternative prescription in rule 40(a) for changing the course with the aid of a postponement. This is the more humane method, and it should always be used. But when a big regatta of say fifteen different classes gets rolling, the committee normally requires something of at least the authority of a Congressional Investigating Committee to convince it to break the starting routine.

Such a committee may have a perfectly sound reason for not postponing; and since this is the sort of thing that doesn't occur to the racing man, let us just spell it out. Suppose short courses have been set in light airs and several classes have started, when suddenly the wind comes in strong from a new direction. The old courses, as set, are too short, and worse still they now contain no windward legs. But to start fifteen classes at five minute intervals requires an hour and a quarter. The boats that started first are bowling around their tiny courses in the brisk breeze, and will be home soon. A postponement now will mean that they'll be finishing before the last classes start. There may be fouls and perhaps serious accidents, the committee will be shorthanded trying to start one race while finishing another, something is sure to go wrong, and the committee will catch general hell from the racing fleet. So in desperation they change the course without postponing, and catch hell anyway. If they did not change it at all they would be even more severely criticized. I can hear the skippers from here: "Why did those boneheads let us sail around reaching courses after the wind shifted?" It is clear to see that if you are a race committee chairman you can't win; don't accept the job unless you are a really dedicated soul.

Another thing the race committee may do unexpectedly is to shorten the course—for any reason. There is usually nothing to be done about this, but once in a while it may make a difference in your tactics. If you are approaching a leeward mark and someone is overtaking you to windward, you must at all costs prevent his establishing an overlap before the mark is reached. But if this mark turns out to be the finish line it makes no difference whether he gets his overlap; the important thing now is only to keep your bow ahead of his. If the committee boat is hanging around as you approach a mark of the course, try to check it for any unusual signals that might indicate that here is the finish line.

This brings me to a point about which I have very positive views, and this time they are not in agreement with current race committee opinion on the subject. International Rule 8, Sec. 1, reads: "In the event of unfavourable conditions of wind, weather, tide or for any other valid reason, the sailing committee may at their discretion shorten the course either before the start of a race or during it." This wording allows the race committee reasonable discretionary powers but does not put any mad ideas into their heads. Contrast to this the wording of the corresponding North American rule (41): ". . . and may cancel or shorten a race while it is in progress because of foul weather endangering the yachts, or light airs making a finish within the time limit unlikely, . . ." It is the words "or shorten" that constitute the Ethiopian in the fuel supply. Here is another committee man's rule if ever there was one. What, pray tell, is the purpose of a time limit? Any racing skipper will tell you: "To protect skippers from having to finish races in extremely light airs, because such airs are always so fluky that it is better that those races should not count in the series score." Thus this rule, allowing the course to be shortened on such a day, exactly defeats the purpose of the time limit. But the race committee man has an altogether different answer. "I never even thought of that," he says. "The purpose of the time limit is to get people

Bermuda News Bureau

K-5 squeezes past the anchor line of the committee boat for the best start.

Nina Lyon

No. 3130 gets away on the port tack into undisturbed air.

home for dinner! If we had no time limit, you'd have to stay out there all night trying to finish. Now, if after a lot of hard work you get only half way around the course by eventide, why not let us establish the finish at the halfway mark? Then you will have a race under your belts instead of no race, we will have somebody to whom to award the prizes that our Prize Committee spent so much time and effort procuring, and the press will have a regatta to report." I warned you that race committees didn't think like human be—beg pardon, like racing skippers.

There is no way to combat the dreadful theory, so incomprehensible to skippers, that a woefully bad race is better than no race. The only point to remember is that it may happen: don't give up and sail home after calculating (correctly) that the race can't finish in time, because if they shorten, it will finish in time, and you will rack up a goose-egg for absenteeism at the finish line.

Here is an entry from one of my race records: "The starting gun failed to go off, and when they blew a whistle instead, we took it for a recall and went back. We later found out that we had made a perfect start and that no one was recalled." We had expected a gun; the unexpected whistle caught us off base.

Another one: "I had set my watch by the race committee's chronometer in the morning. How could I guess that they were going to re-set the chronometer before the race?" The occasion for this unintentional double-cross by the committee was a race in strange waters with a committee whom I did not know. The Stars were first on the program and the interval between guns was only three minutes. It occurred to me that it would be very helpful if we could set our stopwatches accurately on the first preparatory gun, so that we would not be forced to wait until our warning to get the exact time. Three minutes before the start is no time to be fooling with stopwatches. So I ferreted out the chronometer earlier in the day, and everything would have worked out beautifully except for the unexpected contretemps already mentioned. My shrewd idea went for naught as we were left to pick up the signals as best we could, along with everyone else.

It is the duty of the crew as well as of the skipper to keep alert. Frequently the skipper is so busy that a member of the crew has a much better opportunity to look around and to predict awkward situations before they develop. More than one race has been saved for me by a crew who saw that a long string of barges would converge with us in ten or fifteen minutes; thus we were able to plan early and avoid being cut off. On one occasion we were not so smart, and failed to observe in time a submarine coming toward us (on the surface) on a collison course. Since we were already laying the mark, we couldn't come about without throwing away the race. We were hoping that the sub might submerge and pass under us—which would have made a much better story. But instead, the kind captain stopped the ship, and finally rang "astern all engines." I doubt if very many U.S. naval vessels have gone into full reverse for a 22-foot sailboat, but I was heartily in favor of it at the time. A letter to the commandant of the New London Undersea Base expressing our appreciation remains unanswered. Perhaps the Navy would prefer to forget the whole incident.

Alertness pays extra big dividends when there is fog—and I mean more than just the usual amount that occupies the space between the skipper's ears. If you are on a run or a broad reach when the visibility suddenly shuts down, keep a sharp lookout for the next mark to leeward. It is a natural tendency to luff out a bit high of the course on any offwind leg; when the landmarks disappear, this tendency becomes correspondingly harder to combat. In nearly every such instance you will sail almost past the mark before someone discovers it—bearing abeam under the main boom.

1st Mark

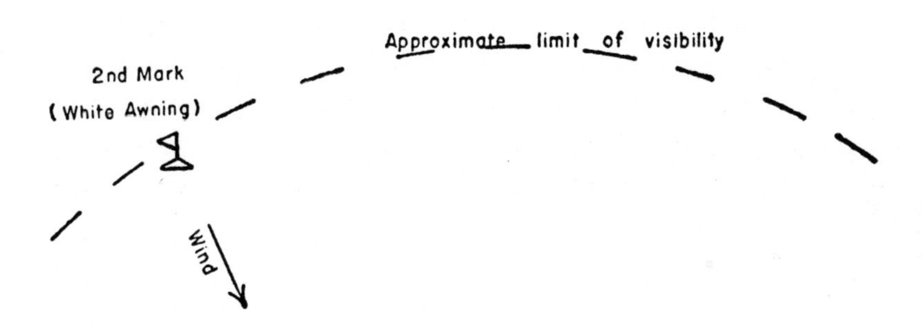

Figure 1. First race at Toronto, 1952.

Two classic examples of the kind of thing we have been talking about in this chapter occurred in the Star Class North American Championship in Toronto in 1952. As we sailed to the starting area for the first race of a three-race series, there was enough haze so that we were soon out of sight of land. We followed the committee boat and her brood of marker yachts and spectator boats, and were among the first Stars there when the line was established. Shortly thereafter, two auxiliary sail boats under power, each towing a stakeboat, took off to windward. These were to be the two marks of a triangular course, and the yachts which towed them were to stand by their respective marks. All this was as advertised according to the circular and it took place on schedule. The only hitch was that *both* boats went nearly to windward, one a little to port and the other a little to starboard of dead into the wind. They looked pretty much alike, too; but we noted that the port one had a white awning over the cockpit. I remarked to my crew, "We'll have to be careful not to mistake that one for the first mark"; we already knew by the way the line was set that all marks were to be left to port.

Pretty soon the port-side boat came to roost, hardly more than a mile away; the white awning was clearly visible whenever the fog was not too soupy. Meanwhile the starboard boat had disappeared and, to make matters worse, the wind hauled a point or so before gun time, so that our friend of the white awning was now almost dead to windward of the starting line (see Fig. 1). It was too close to be the weather mark according to the published instructions; but it was also too tempting: twenty-five of the thirty entries went there!

They had not seen the other mark go out to the right; we had. Nevertheless when five-sixths of a fleet of nationally known experts goes one way, it takes a certain amount of intestinal fortitude to go the other, and it was a mighty lonely contingent of five boats which we led away into the fog on the port tack.

But we were bound and determined to stay on the port tack until that other mark showed up, which of course it finally did —dead ahead. By this time the leaders of the majority party up under the beach had sighted land, and realized that if they were going to leave White Awning to port, the next mark would have to be in the middle of a wheat field. At about this juncture the fog lifted enough for them to see us—and the situation—all too clearly. The procession which now trudged past us on the way to the right first mark as we sailed to the second was indeed a doleful one. We won by a large margin, with most of the best competition finishing down the drain.

We hardly expected this race to stand, but it did. Nobody could think of a valid excuse for disallowing it. The second race was normal, in a steady strong breeze, and *Flame* salvaged a fourth. For the third race it blew even harder. We had only two points of our pirated lead left, so that another fourth could lose the series. But now came the second deciding break. In the strong northeaster, the stakeboat marking the starboard end of the line would not stay put. About twenty minutes before the start the race committee sent out its launch to tow the stakeboat to windward, and, anticipating that it would drag again, they took it a little too far to windward. The competitors of course saw all this, and began to congregate at the now favored starboard end. What they did not see was that, even as the committee expected, it began slowly to drag again. About six minutes before starting time they decided to try once more to straighten up the line. This was perhaps an error: the line would have been poor but possible if left alone. What actually happened was that the stakeboat's anchor rope fouled the launch's propeller, and the two of them drifted in a tangle much faster than before. Moreover, many competitors lost sight of the stakeboat altogether in the flying spray and confusion as it lay alongside of and half hidden by the launch. By gunfire the stakeboat was a long, long way to leeward of the committee boat (Fig. 2); and all but two Stars were still down there or beating their way up, too late, toward the now greatly favored committee end. *Flame* started on the gun, ten feet from the committee boat, on the port tack (the line could no longer be crossed on starboard), in company with exactly one other Star.* This bit of grand larceny permitted us to round the first mark first and finish the race third, for a very close series victory against several potentially superior skippers who had sailed themselves out of the series through failure to expect the unexpected.

One last word on the subject of fouled-up races. Sometimes a harassed race committee, when faced with an apparently insoluble problem involving whether to let a race stand or throw it out and schedule a re-sail, will say, as a last resort: "We can't decide; we'll throw it open to a vote of the skippers." Gentlemen of the race committee, please don't be so naive. When you do this you have in effect already decided: there will be a re-sail. Obviously a majority, possibly three-quarters, of the skippers in *any* race are dissatisfied with their finish positions and would be delighted to have another chance. Putting the question of a re-sail to a vote of the skippers not only works an injustice on the minority who led the fleet; adding insult to injury, it makes them look like heels for wanting the race to stand. So, Mr. Chairman, if you can't decide and are about to ask for a skippers' vote, pause and realize that you have already decided. Announce a re-sail. You are now a strong man who is willing to admit he has made a mistake and wishes to put it right, instead of a weak one who can't make up his own mind what to do next. Your stock will rise instead of falling in the opinion of the racing skippers—and you will be doing what they would have voted for anyway.

* Former World's Champion Arthur M. Deacon, one of the most observant skippers in the game.

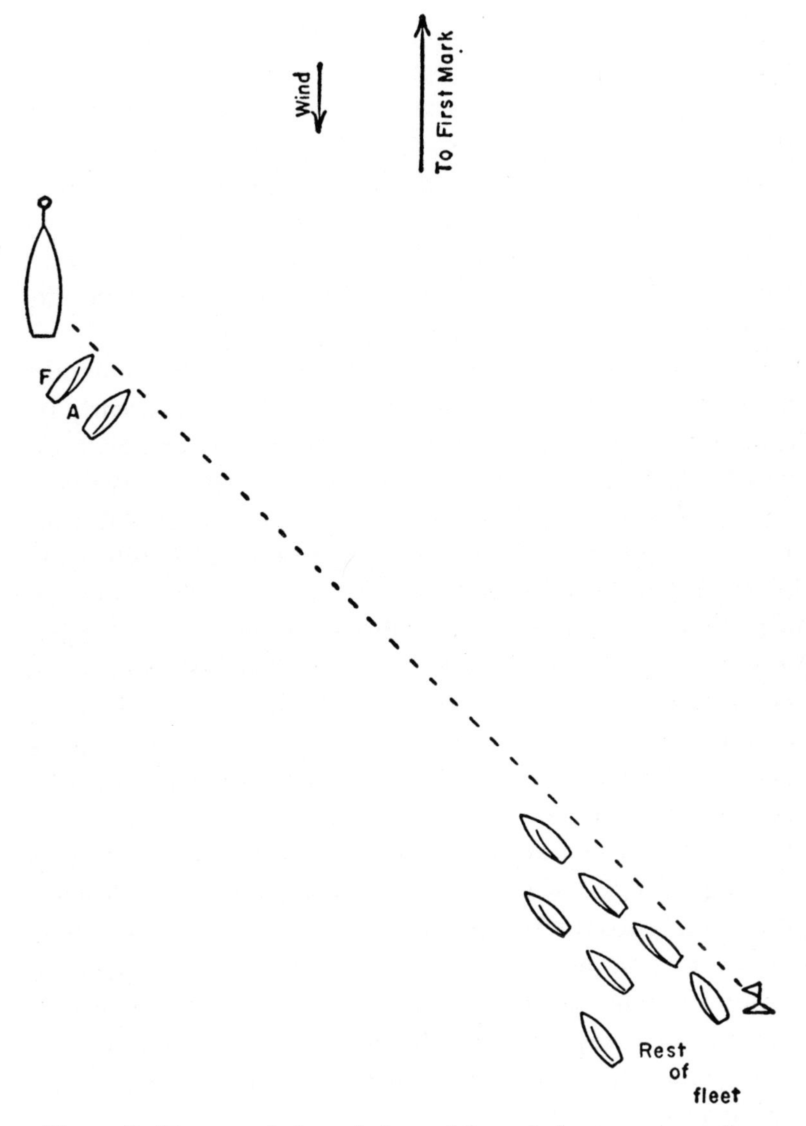

Figure 2. *Flame* and *Armade* have things their own way at the weather end.

CHAPTER 4

Starting Tactics

There are few thrills in yacht racing comparable to that of leading the fleet across the starting line. A feeling of accomplishment out of proportion to the advantage gained in the race seems to be the reward of a spectacular first start. Certain skippers in each class are past masters in the art of starting: you can count on them to put on a good show every time, and they usually get away with it.

Maybe I am getting old and conservative, because I find myself making fewer hair-raising starts than in the past. There was a time when every line not laid out perfectly square to the wind (and few lines are), presented a challenge. "We'll have to start right at the flag," I'd say, "on the gun." Sometimes we'd foul out; sometimes we'd get recalled; often, of course, we'd be out-maneuvered and someone else would get the coveted best slot. Once in a while we'd pull it off and *Flame* would be away in the lead.

Not so nowadays. We follow a different plan. Not only is it less conducive to ulcers, but it produces better results. I don't claim that this "system" is in any way original: doubtless many experts have been using it for years. It is a method of trying not for the best start but for the *second best* start. The interesting point is that the boat that gets the second start usually starts not alongside the boat in first place but somewhere else entirely.

Only one boat can get *the* first start. It is the start made by the skipper who, with his heart in his mouth, squeezes past the anchor line of the stakeboat or the committee boat as the gun is fired. (See page 20.) For one thing, this skipper incurs a serious risk of getting recalled or fouling out; for another, if his start fails for any reason, he has no easy way out of his difficulty. By the time he is on the favored spot he is so surrounded by boats that he has no margin for error, nowhere to go if things go wrong. If he arrives two seconds too early he has no room to kill way, and the consequent recall is a costly one because the surrounding area is so crowded. If he is five seconds too late, someone else will secure the favored berth. "That's not so bad," you may think; "he can get *almost* the best start." But that's just what doesn't happen. A second-best start of that kind does not last, for reasons of backwind and disturbed air. You soon find yourself pinching the boat, with little headway and no means of escape.

Where to start, then? The middle of the line is not good, because it is too difficult to judge exactly where the line lies, so that the margin between a safe start and a possible recall is too large. You are very much on your own out there: it is generally impossible to hear your number if you are recalled. Besides, you may not be willing to sacrifice the distance to windward lost by a middle position if one end is strongly favored. A better place is about one quarter of the way down the line from the end which you consider the preferred one. If you start here, one other boat will, at a considerable risk, make a start better than yours at the extreme end of the line. But you may be surprised to discover that you are almost immediately second to him in the race, having quickly overtaken the hapless group who tried for a "best" start but didn't quite make it. A safe second start is much more to be desired than a precarious first one.

An exception to the rule of not starting in the middle of the line can occur under a system occasionally used by some enlightened committees. In a large fleet a good line must be very long indeed; and to help the skippers find the middle of it a control flag is placed there, to mark the line but not to constitute a mark of the course. Such a flag is a great help to anyone who happens to want to start near it. Presumably you would do so only if the line were square to the wind.

A smartly executed port tack start is often a fine "second best." For some reason, race committees tend to lay out the line so that the port end (so-called leeward end) is slightly favored. In this case there is always a jam of starboard tack boats at that end; but as we have observed, only one of them can get away in clear air. It is obviously suicidal to attempt a port tack start *at* the favored end: you would only end up with a bisected boat. Instead, you should now reach along the line on port tack and shoot through the first available "hole" between two starboard tackers. There is pretty sure to be such a hole eventually; and you must not mind bearing off under a lot of sterns to find it, because all the time you are doing so you are moving at a good fast pace, much faster than the starboard boats who are stamping and pinching in each others' disturbed air and water. When you finally get away you carry your good head of steam for several seconds, and what is much more important, you are in clear air all by yourself. (Fig. 3.) Furthermore, when you next converge with the fleet, you will be on starboard tack, they on port. You should be well up in the money at that stage—quite possibly in first place.

There are times when a port tack start is the one to take even if it means crossing under the entire fleet. These are special occasions, to be sure; but as we remarked in the last chapter, many series are won or lost on special occasions. Suppose the first leg is not a perfectly dead beat to windward, but one which consists of very long port boards and very short starboard ones. It may now be fatal to start on the starboard tack—but you can be sure that everyone will do so! If there is the slightest chance of laying the first mark on the port tack from the starting area, or even if you can come close to laying it,

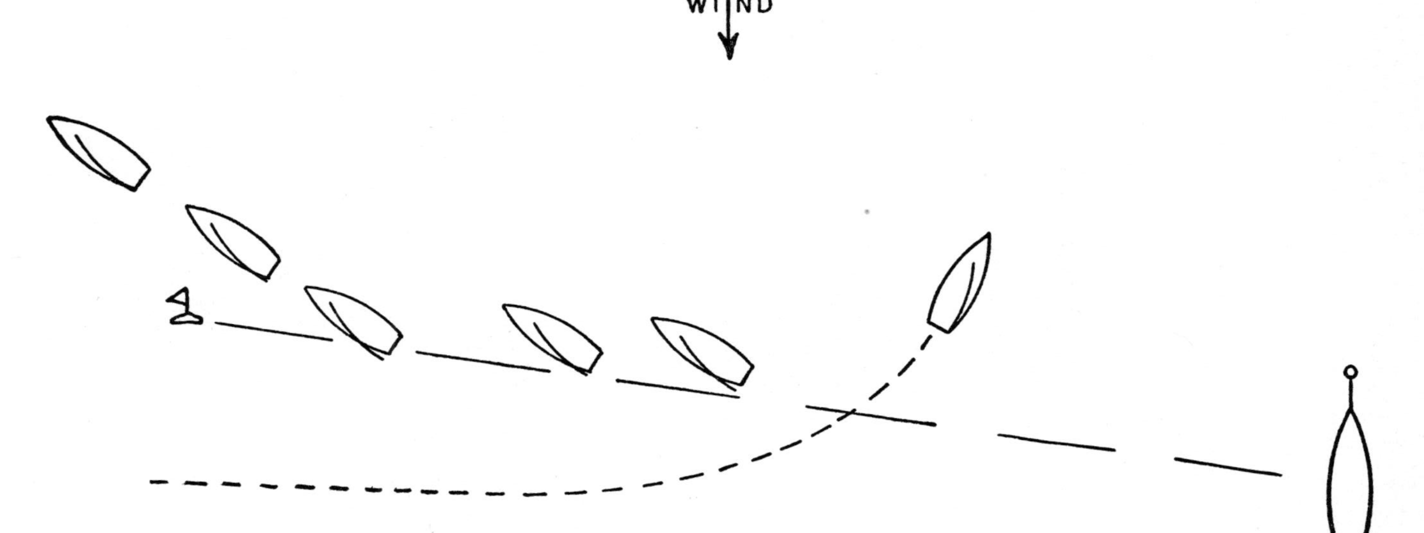

Figure 3. The port tack boat has clear air.

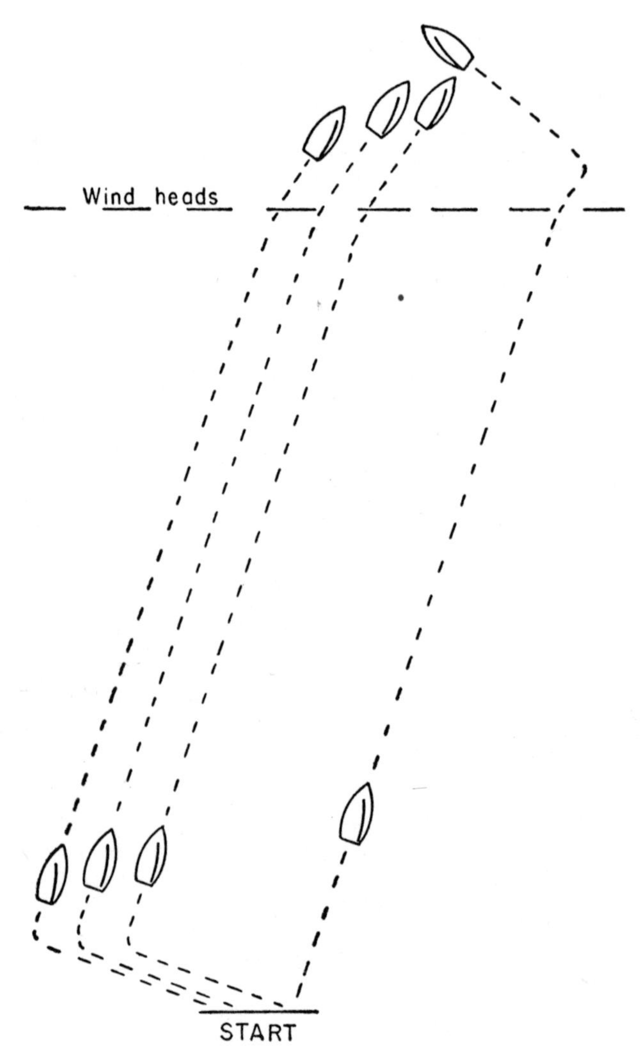

Figure 4. The boat that started on port tack crosses the fleet on a header.

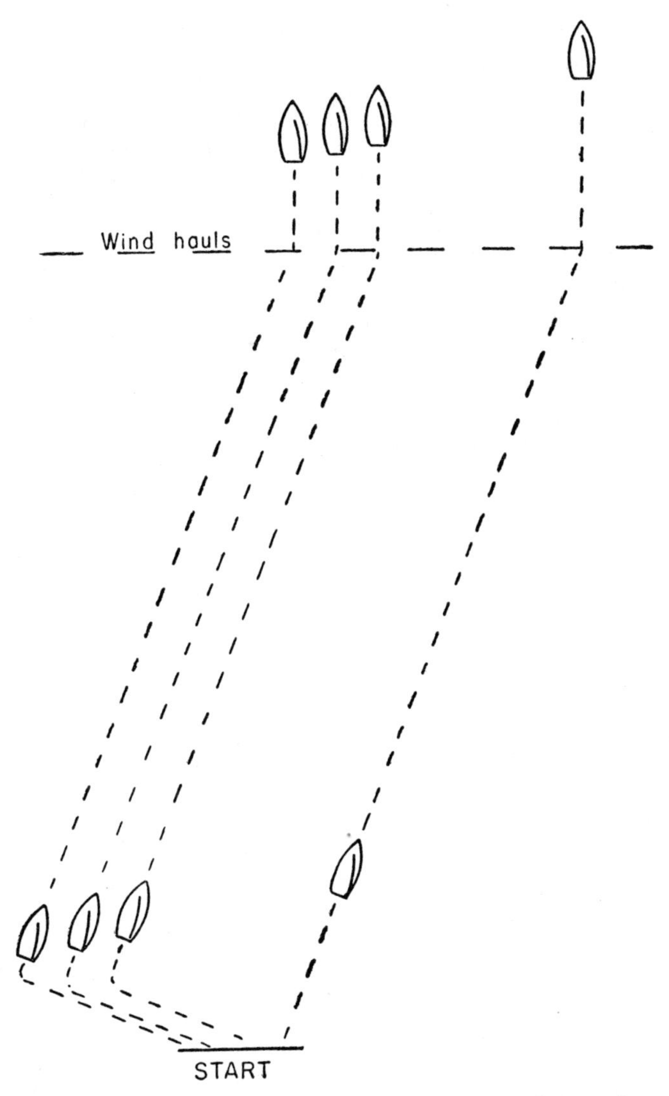

Figure 5. The boat that started on port tack lays the mark on a let-up.

you should cross the line on the port tack, I don't care where. Under these conditions, every yard sailed on the starboard tack may be a yard wasted. Stay on the port tack until you near the mark. All the way up the leg you are sitting pretty: if the wind heads you can tack and cross the fleet, (Fig. 4), and if it hauls you will lay the mark and everybody else will overstand (Fig. 5). The one condition under which you might fail to gain back all you lost at the start and more is a perfectly steady wind; and the wind is hardly likely to be steady in this race. It was probably the unsteady character of the wind that caused the course to turn out lop-sided in the first place. Even in the unlikely contingency that it is steady, you will hold the commanding starboard tack position when you approach the mark.

Whenever all buoys are to be left to port the committee boat marks the starboard end of the line. If the boat is a big one, like the sizable Coast Cuard cutters frequently used at major small-boat regattas, another special condition can develop. The recommended start may this time give you a gray hair or two; but it is not as difficult as it sounds. The two situations described under this category may not occur once a season in races in which you participate; but when they do they are easily recognized.

Suppose the line favors the starboard end and the white flag is somewhere forward of amidships on a long committee boat—perhaps on the flying bridge, a favorite spot with race committees. There is bound to be a crowd approaching the stern of the committee boat shortly before gunfire, everyone trying to attain the weather berth, we trust without barging. There is a start which will beat them all, and if the committee boat happens to be lying at a slight angle because of a current set, the maneuver can be carried out safely with almost no risk of a foul. You approach the line from the wrong side, passing to weather of the anchored vessel (Boat *A* in Fig. 6). There is a triangular area into which the yachts that come up in the

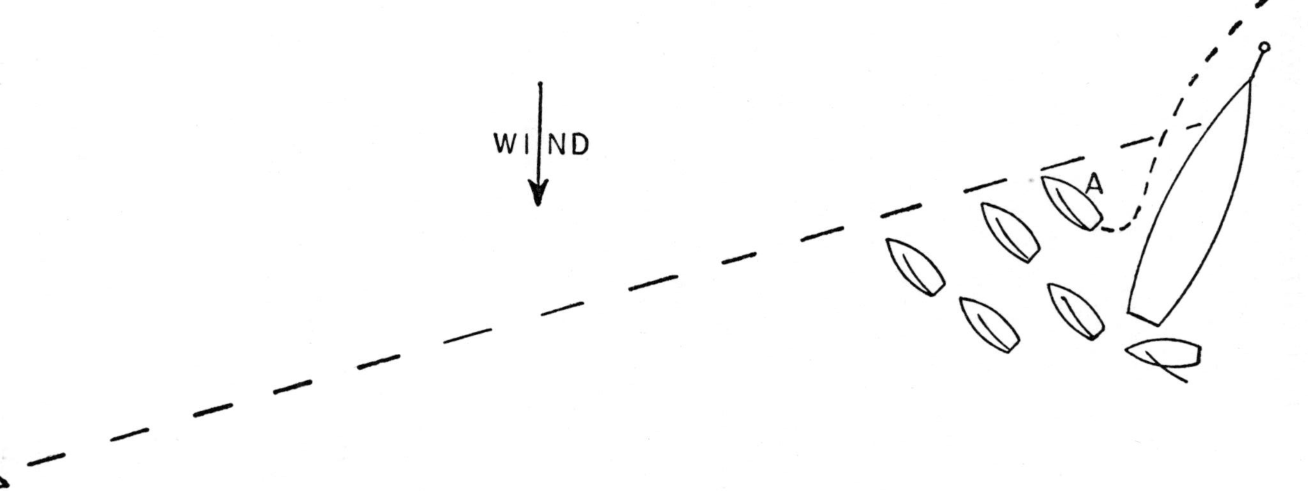

Figure 6. Boat *A* gets the first start.

normal manner simply cannot sail, and it is in this area that you turn to cross the line in the lead, leaving the rest of the fleet wondering how in thunder you got there. Two things can go wrong: you can arrive too late, in which case you make merely a good start but not necessarily the best; or you can arrive too early, in which case your troubles are more serious but not insurmountable. You can't bear off and wait, because you would be barging in full view of the committee, and besides would very likely run into somebody. The only alternative is to go through with it and get yourself recalled. Even then you may be able to circle around immediately and do exactly the same start over again. At any rate, none of these things happen if your timing is right.

The second case is similar but even more spectacular, and it too requires perfect timing. The line layout is much the same, and you start in the same spot; but the committee boat doesn't happen to be angled this time, so you get there differently. Sail up into the triangle on the port tack (nobody will be in your way because it is still a few seconds until gunfire), and tack at about the instant when that old boy up on the committee boat is dodging to keep his yachting cap from being knocked off by your starboard spreader (Fig. 7). If it isn't blowing too hard, both of these starts will be facilitated by the fact that you are only a few feet away from the officials and can hear them counting out the last seconds of time remaining before gunfire. It is well to check the location of the cannon: the wad of the blank cartridge has been known to go right through a mainsail.

These two starts are not merely hypothetical ones, the figments of an imagination deranged by too much scheming and plotting to win sailboat races. The first was a favorite of former Lightning wizard, Jack Webb of Riverside, Connecticut; the second was recommended to me by Stanley Barnes, the International 110 expert, who has succeeded in getting away with it more than once. In the opening race of the 1956 Star Class

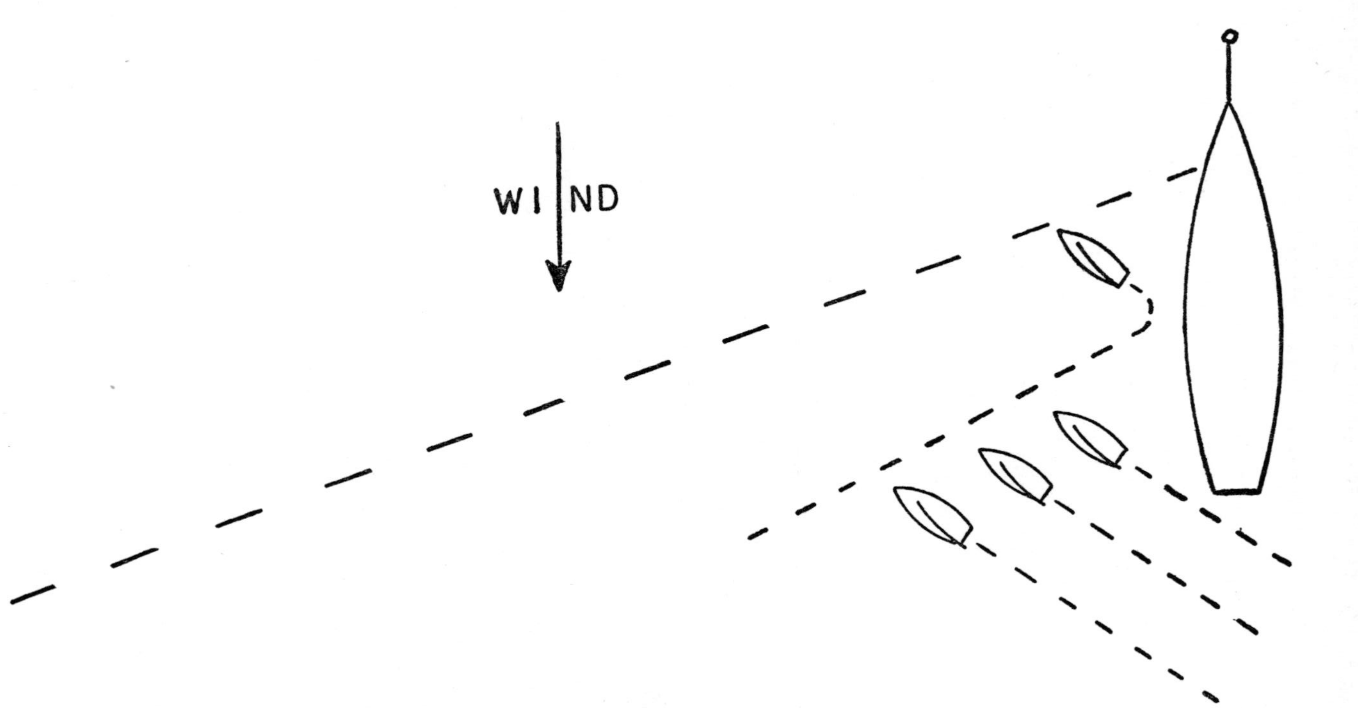

Figure 7. Another first start stolen from "coffin corner."

World's Championship at Naples, in a fleet of 59 boats, Harry G. Nye, Jr., of Chicago, developed a variation of this start and pulled it off with great success. He sailed downwind from the wrong side of the line into the empty triangle, made a U-turn in front of the pack, and started on the port tack under the noses of the committee, with room to spare. The picture facing page 21 shows him getting away in clear air. Port was the tack to pursue that day, and he knew it: by going in the right direction before anyone else had had time to get organized, he won the race.

The most frightening jams of all occur when the starboard (windward) end is favored. Now there is no choice but to start on the starboard tack, and everyone does. Further, everyone crowds the weather end, and despite the anti-barging rule there are often infringements. A good device in this case is to wait a bit. Plan to arrive at the desired weather berth, but be a few seconds late. You may be surprised what happens. Because the eager beavers are a shade early, they may have to bear off before gunfire, leaving you a perfect hole. Even if they should hit it right and you are forced to cross in their wakes, you should be close enough to the end of the line to tack immediately, to clear your air. You will probably be the only boat in a position to do that; it is worth being a few seconds late for the privilege.

It very often happens that the wind around the starting area goes dead just before the racc starts. (We shall return to an analysis of the reasons for this phenomenon in a later chapter.) Therefore it is a cardinal principle, especially on light days, to get out to the line early and stay there. It is surely most distressing to start the race with a handicap of several minutes because you were away taking a swim too near race time.

Keep close track of the race committee, especially when racing in strange waters. Most of us are spoiled by race committees which are too kind to us. They announce a start for *X* o'clock, but if the boats are still struggling out from their moorings, come *X* o'clock a postponement will be signalled to wait for the crowd to arrive. Don't count on that postponement! Some committees won't operate that way. I recall only too well a race on Chesapeake Bay in which most of the fleet were caught off-balance by a punctual committee. The morning race had been delayed by a thundersquall with rain so heavy that it had reduced the visibility to the danger point. On the completion of that race at about 1:00 P.M. everybody came ashore for lunch and to dry out, which was as per schedule. At 1:50 a gun was fired from the committee boat, now anchored in plain sight not 200 yards from the clubhouse. Some competitors, if they noticed the gun at all, took it for a preliminary attention signal, a "Hey, fellows, come on out here and let's get the show under way." On the contrary, it was the preparatory gun for the afternoon race, right on schedule. Another gun went off, and still many contestants were making leisurely preparations to leave their moorings. N.B.: Any boat still made fast to a buoy after the 5-minute gun is actually disqualified (NAYRU rule 31, IYRU rule 23,1). This rule, like many others, is frequently violated unintentionally and in ignorance of the existence of such a rule.

On the *Flame* we were rudely awakened to the facts of life just as we were casting off, by a young damsel in a Penguin who sweetly informed us that our class started in thirty seconds. There was a good breeze blowing and we covered 200 yards in record time—but we couldn't make it in thirty seconds. We arrived forty-five seconds late; but the rest of the fleet was in such a dither that nearly everyone started at the wrong end of the line. We, of course, crossed at the nearest available spot, which happened to be the right end, and made a passable start by the sheerest of undeserved good luck. At this point my crew remarked, "Cheer up; Bob [our most dangerous competitor] is just getting his mainsail out of the bag." He crossed the line 4½ minutes later in a pall of gloom.

I raced in the same regatta the following year. Determined to avoid another such fiasco we took lunch with us and never left the starting area between races. But the committee did: it had to go away to start another regatta during lunch hour, and the chairman hailed us as they pulled off, saying "We'll be back in time to start you on schedule." Well, he wasn't; but he started us on schedule anyway! He anchored the committee boat before it had reached the old starting area and established a new one, rather than postpone. Again many boats were late, and again we only just made it (legally this time). Maybe against such a committee you just can't win. These are unusual cases: most committees delay too much rather than too little. But they illustrate again the point that can hardly be emphasized too often: you must be prepared for anything in yacht racing.

After most of this chapter had been written I heard from a friend who was a victim of it, that the same committee, in a major regatta held later the same year, was responsible for the following debacle. In a very hard northwester the committee boat proceeded to the starting area, followed by twenty wallowing sailboats. There they fired two guns and displayed code flag *C,* which according to the printed race circular was the signal meaning "Race Called Off." Thereupon the boat upped anchor and returned past the club anchorage, proceeding on up the river until out of sight. Six boats dropped out of the cavalcade and made their moorings, logically enough. The rest, for reasons best known to themselves, followed the committee boat up the river. When sheltered water was reached a starting line was established and the race sailed. Upon its subsequent return to civilization, the committee was greatly shocked to be handed a formal protest demanding that the race be disallowed.

I mention this incident not in a fit of pique (I wasn't even there), but only in the forlorn hope that some day some committee man may chance to read it. Race committees are prone to be a trifle intolerant of skippers who mis-read, mistake or fail to observe posted signals. It would therefore seem only fair that they themselves should be meticulously correct in their handling of the signals. Racing skippers are obliged to be ever alert for all possible signals, and under conditions of physical stress and difficult visibility must be able to pick up unexpected and surprise changes without warning, reading their meaning from a soggy and perhaps mutilated circular and interpreting it instantly without time for contemplation or study. Is it unreasonable for the skipper to feel that the least the committee can do is not to bungle their end of it? With all the time they choose to take, with a supply of clean fresh circulars to consult, in a warm dry cabin, with a rule book at one elbow and a subordinate to carry out orders at the other, is it too much to ask that the committee hoist visible signals that mean what they say, and then follow their own instructions?

CHAPTER 5

To Windward In Unsteady Breezes

One philosophy of sailboat racing—and there are many good skippers who subscribe to it—contends that the most important part of the game, the skill which one should try to develop above anything else, is the ability to take a boat to windward in a steady breeze. The idea is that if you can win all the knock-down drag-out battles, you'll come out on top for the season. Inherent in this philosophy is the implication that this sort of race is also the *best* race—the truest test and the most fun. With this last idea I shall not quarrel. The strong steady breeze with the "ideal" windward leg is of course the best test—of something; to be exact, it tests who can sail fastest in a strong steady breeze over an ideal windward leg. As for what is the most fun, who can say? Certainly everyone is entitled to his own opinion on that, and the finest sailing day of the summer for one man may keep another tied up at his mooring. What I must vigorously oppose, however, is the first theory: that ability to move the boat to windward in a steady breeze is of maximum *importance*. Esthetically it may be; practically it just isn't so.

You have read enough of this book by now to know that I don't believe series are won that way. This opinion is based not on experience in only one (fluky) locality. A long and checkered sailing career has taken me to forty different racing areas in eight countries. The propaganda put out by my sailing friends in most of these places, either to entice people into visiting them or simply on general principles, includes glowing descriptions of their fine steady breezes. You know how it goes: "You can set your watch by the 20-knot afternoon southerly that strikes in at two o'clock every day." Let me warn you that if you do, your watch will become a pretty unreliable timepiece. I admit that I have not yet tried Buzzards Bay or San Francisco Bay; but at every other one of the famous "heavy weather" places in this country in recent years the heavy weather has turned out to be a myth. As for the light weather places, the less said about them the better.

What all this adds up to is that ability to sail to windward in a good steady breeze may be laudable and it may be fun, but it isn't fair to label it *the most important* desideratum, for the simple reason that it doesn't win series. If our criterion is to be success in series, we must realize that the unsteady breezes, by their sheer weight of numbers, are the more important ones to understand and to learn how to handle.

Trevor and Calahan pointed out, in a book published many years ago,* that even the supposedly steady winds are not steady at all, but contain substantial shifts. I do not wish to labor this point, because what I am interested in is a technique for the very shifty breezes. In that book was a reproduction of an anemograph, the record of wind direction made while a northwester was blowing. The graph was never steady; the recording pen described very rapid oscillations of four points or more all afternoon.

Northwesters are the typical shifty breeze of the North American continent. No one knows quite what makes them behave the way they do. On the United States eastern seaboard the northwester is shifty partly because it is a land breeze; but there are other land breezes (the strong westerly, for example), that are much steadier. Furthermore, a northwester is equally shifty on the south shore of Lake Erie where it has just arrived across 80 miles of open water. In some localities the southwest breeze is unsteady. Off the Chicago waterfront the southwester

* WIND AND TIDE IN YACHT RACING, by H. A. Calahan and J. B. Trevor, Harcourt Brace & Co., New York, 1936.

takes such a beating getting through the heat and canyons of the city that it swings back and forth through a considerable arc over southern Lake Michigan. On small lakes almost no breeze is steady. For brevity, however, let us catalog all breezes of this type under the name of northwesters.

About a page of SUCCESSFUL YACHT RACING was devoted to explaining what happens when you capitalize on the windshifts of a northwester. Apparently one page was not nearly enough. Most people do not understand how to handle these breezes, and the reason they don't is that they fail to grasp the notion of *tacking on headers.* If you do understand this principle you may skip the next paragraph.

Take the most extreme example possible. Suppose two boats are beating to a windward mark. Boat *A* is just laying the mark on the starboard tack and Boat *B* is still on the port tack (Fig. 8). Suppose now the wind shifts counterclockwise through eight points (90°), and that, at the same time, both boats tack. The situation has now become that of Figure 9: Boat *A* is still sailing straight toward the mark, and Boat *B* is again sailing on a (different) course that takes her no nearer the mark. Obviously if this procedure were repeated in another shift of wind through eight points clockwise with both boats tacking again, and then repeated again, and so on, Boat *A* would soon reach the mark in a straight line; but the hapless Boat *B* would sail back and forth all day, never getting any nearer the mark.

This is the ultimate illustration of the advantage of tacking when you are headed. Of course we don't normally get 90° wind shifts; and the skipper of Boat *B* would never stay on the tack that failed to take him toward the mark when he saw that the other tack would do so. But if we modify the situation down to shifts of four points, or two points, or indeed *any shifts at all,* the same principle holds: *Whenever you get headed, tack.* And if by any chance the wind lets you up, even if you were about to tack, don't: wait for it to head again, which it will if it's that

Mark

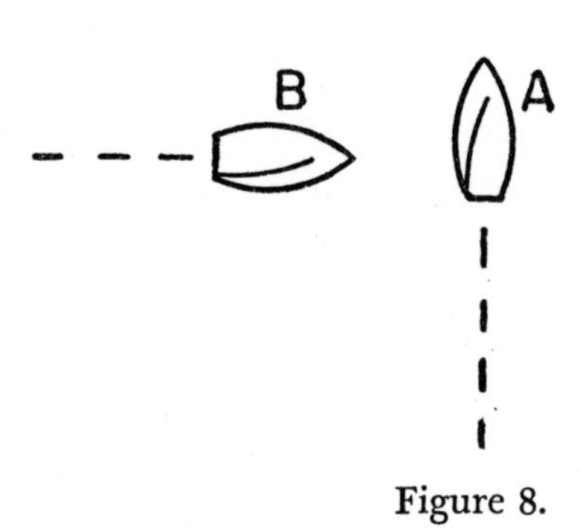

Figure 8.

kind of day; and then tack. If you tack when you have just been favored by a let-up you are behaving, to a more or less modified degree, like Boat *B*.

The point which even many experts miss is that the gains made by tacking on headers are not small; they are enormous. In the above-mentioned book some specific calculations were described. It was assumed that the wind on a certain day might pendulum back and forth through a total swing of two points (22½°), certainly a modest assumption. Northwesters commonly oscillate through a much wider arc than that. Then, over a windward leg only three miles long, Boat *A* was assumed to tack correctly on all the headers, whereas Boat *B* made all the mistakes and tacked every time she was let up. It turned out that *A* beat *B* to the mark *by eighteen minutes.* If both boats traveled at the same speed through the water, *B* had to travel almost 50% farther than *A* to reach the mark.

It should hardly be necessary to emphasize that when this sort of thing is going on it is silly to think about anything else. On northwest days there is so much action, so many fast tacks and double tacks, that you can sail half the weather leg trimmed wrong, because you don't have time to find out what trim is exactly right, and still get to the windward mark so far ahead that the race is in the bag. I have often arrived at the weather mark of such a race literally breathless.

Because they don't understand shifty breezes, many skippers don't like them. They think winning in breezes that swing back and forth is all luck. It's not luck, but method. You can learn how to sail in a northwester just as definitely and systematically as you can learn any other specialty of yacht racing. But those who worship steady weather, who believe there is no merit in winning under any other conditions, never get the hang of northwesters. After the race you hear them moaning: "The first time upwind the westerly tack won out; so the second time up I went west and everybody on the northerly tack

Mark

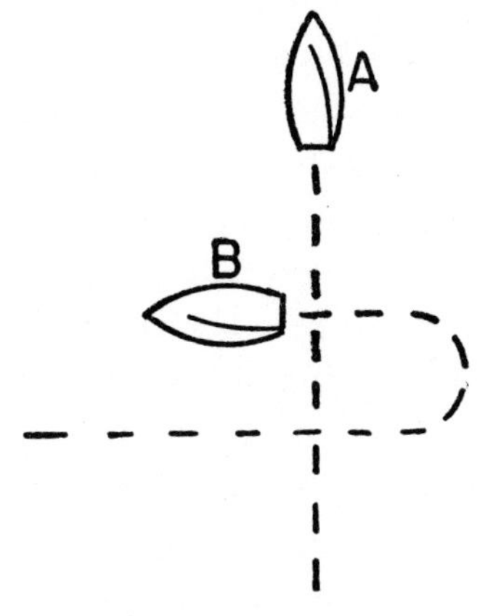

Figure 9.

whaled us. What can you do on a day like that?" I can tell them what they should (but don't) do: get out a pencil and paper and start drawing a few simple diagrams of what's been happening to them. A complaint like the above reveals real lack of understanding of the way in which a northwester operates. Indeed, the very fact that the westerly boats were favored the first time up may be a strong signal to go north, not west, the next time, as we shall presently see.

There are many occasions when you find yourself sailing the same weather leg twice (or more) on the same day. The most frequent occurrence of this is in a twice-around course; but it happens also in dinghy racing, intercollegiate regattas, round robins and the like, whenever several short races are sailed in the course of a single afternoon. On a northwest day the first windward leg usually gives at least a hint and often a sure-fire prescription how to sail the second one. On this kind of day one tack normally takes you nearer the mark than the other because the wind is seldom blowing straight from the mark to you. Thus even at the start there is a preferred tack. You have to watch for it very carefully, because the shifts occur so rapidly that the wind direction may change two, three or four points in the last thirty seconds before your start. At any rate you must get on the preferred tack and make an immediate mental note of your heading against the distant shore or take a compass bearing if there is no shore. This is now filed for reference. You will continue to note whether you hold high on the same tack, and for how long; and when you get headed and go about, you take new readings on the new tack. All this is a record, mental or actual, of your trip up the first leg. It will help you immensely the second time up, because you will then know at a glance, immediately after rounding the home mark, which tack the wind is currently favoring, *even if you can't see the windward mark*. The big error that most skippers make at this stage is to start to windward blindly, not knowing whether they are on the right tack. Often they find out too late that they are on the wrong one.

In my notes I find a description of a race so typical of the northwest day that I am taking the liberty of quoting the whole thing. It illustrates not only the point in question but several others discussed earlier.

"*Sat. Sept. 13, 1952.* 33 entries. Light, rather fishy NW to W. The committee had evidently set the course for W, and when it went to NW before the start they didn't have time to change the course or the line. Result: a feverish jam at the weather (starboard) end. Knowing we must never go onto port tack because we could probably lay the first mark on starboard, we tried to wait and start windward late. But it didn't work: we ended up barging beautifully, and were forced to tack and jibe in a hurry, missing the committee boat by about 6 inches. Hence we made a wretched start, and not being able to tack to clear, we staggered up the first leg in many people's backwinds. Finally, as the mark came into view dead ahead, the wind headed two or three points and the last quarter of the leg was a good beat. We eventually rounded sixth, with the leaders a long way ahead; but we reached fast and rounded the home mark fifth and back in the ball game.

"Second round. The windward leg was now a true beat in a light NW with stronger puffs visible inshore. We reasoned that since it had obviously been all the way north at the start, it was now all the way west, and therefore likely to go back to north if anything. So we took off for the beach, and did get headed, and also picked up a little more air than the outside crowd; we rounded first and won the race."

Observe that those who tacked inshore at the beginning of the leg the *first* time up wound up in the ashcan because the port tack at that time was carrying them at right angles to the direction of the first mark. Yet after this race someone remarked to me, "You sure were lucky, going inshore the second time; I went in there the first time and got shellacked!" When this happens—and it happens all the time—you learn to pass it off with a shrug and agree, "Yes, pretty lucky."

About half of the starts in northwest races come equipped with a built-in booby-trap. The starting line on this kind of day can be square to the direction of the wind only part of the time at best; first one end is favored, then the other. You are supposed to start at the end that is to weather when your gun goes off. If this is the starboard end, well and good: start there and keep sailing until you get headed. But if the favored end happens to be the port or left hand end, look out for trouble. In this case it is all right to start at that end on starboard tack *only if you can tack immediately*. Note that what has made this the preferred end is a swing of the wind toward the west. This is a strong header for the starboard tack boats relative to the average wind direction. You must not stay on the starboard tack during such a header; but it will surely be impossible to tack, unless the header is so extreme that the boat on your weather quarter is almost dead astern. The way out of this trap is not to be lured into the attractive starboard tack start in the first place. Start on port, sacrificing the weather berth to do so. Never mind if you lose a dozen lengths thereby. Let those starboard tackers who crossed your bow stay on that tack for only a very short time and they will have lost more than a dozen lengths. You are sailing away from them on the right tack, and the farther away they let you go, the greater will be your lead after the next windshift. If this is not already perfectly clear to you, it would be well worth your while to study the diagram of Figure 10 until it becomes quite obvious what is happening.

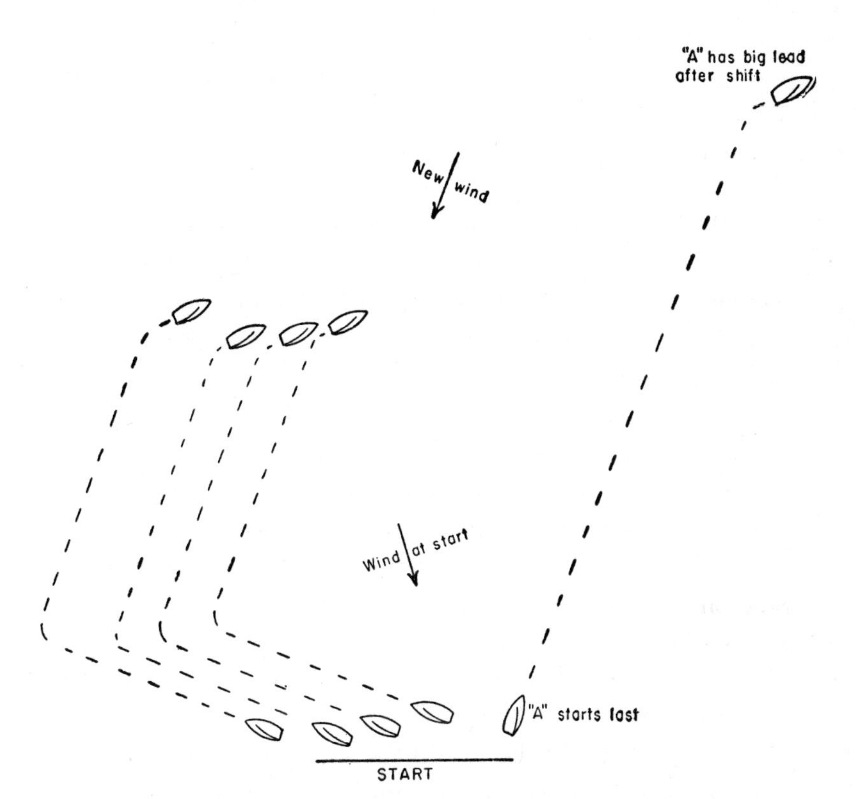

Figure 10. Boat "A" reaps the reward of starting on the right tack.

CHAPTER 6

Sail Your Own Race

In the last few chapters we have mentioned many of the less publicized ways in which races are won. Whether you noticed it or not, all the various and quite different episodes and techniques described had one feature in common: they neglected consideration of the other boats. In some cases the winning plan included the hope that the other boats would all sooner or later make a wrong move; and perhaps it is implicit in any race that the winner could have been beaten by some other boat if it had done all the things the winner did, only a little better. But up till now we have not talked about doing anything to stop another boat from going by. We have not been paying any attention at all to the other boats.

In our quest for the answer to the question of how races are won let us pause for a moment and ask, how are they lost? This is a loaded question, because in a race of 20 boats there is only one winner, and technically I suppose there are 19 losers, and each of the 19 devised his own way of losing. But it is unfair to call the runner-up a "loser" in any sense of the word. He has beaten 18 boats, and his is a well deserved and probably hard earned victory. You are usually quite happy to settle for second. The same can be said for the third or fourth or fifth boat, and one hesitates to draw the line and say, "Below here the boats in this race were badly sailed." Therefore, as usual, we shall have to hedge and modify the question in order to simplify the answer: how can we avoid doing so poorly in so many races?

One of the main causes of doing badly—losing races, if you

Rosenfeld

The wind goes dead around a starting area.

Kalita-Sunpapers

"A mammoth puff dismasted *Flower*."

please—is paying too much attention to the other boats. The full dividends that accrue to alertness and observation are presumably not going to be paid to your competitors because it is your job to be more alert and more observant than they. It is not by watching *them* that you can find out what to do. In fact, you have too much to do already without watching them. Sail your own race and win it and let them go away and sink for all you care.

Yes, I know, there are times when you have to cover. But the fetish of covering is greatly overdone. Races can be lost, dismally, by covering. Sometimes it is foolish not to cover, but often it is equally foolish to do so. Most people would admit that if you have a *good* lead near the *end* of a race it would be folly not to cover. But how often are you in so fortunate a position? This is the exception rather than the rule, and when it happens, the covering will take care of itself: there is no doubt that you will stay between the finish and your most dangerous competitor. But what about other occasions when you find yourself leading the pack?

In most races the lead changes many times. Especially on a fluky day, first one boat assumes the lead, then another, only to be replaced by a third, until finally every boat in the race has had a whack at it. Has it ever occurred to you to wonder why on such a day the fellow who "just happens" to be in the lead at the finish is nearly always one of the top ranking skippers of the fleet? I believe it is because he is the man who knows when and when not to cover. If he gets into the lead early in the race he is not greatly impressed by the fact. He continues to sail his own race, and may lose the lead temporarily on the chance of acquiring a more substantial one later when it counts. On the other hand your novice in first place forgets everything in an attempt to stay ahead of the nearest boat. On a light, fluky day this approach to the problem is usually fatal.

Even on a steady day there is entirely too much covering

done near the beginning of races. Five minutes after the start of the first weather leg, Joe Neophyte looks around and finds to his astonishment that he is in first place. This may be due to any of a dozen different causes, each of which requires a different response in order to maintain or increase the lead. If it was a windshift, he must tack if it is going to shift back, but he must hold on if it is going to head more. Maybe it was not a header at all but a local lift. Perhaps the others are not yet trimmed right and he happens to be. Perhaps he had a better start than he expected. No matter what the cause, *his lead is small* at this stage, and it must be increased, not protected. But Joe is so shook up by his unaccustomed good fortune that he can think of nothing but covering, and after two or three frenzied tacks his little lead has vanished.

By and large it doesn't make sense to cover near the start of the race. You will find none of the experts doing it. They realize that there are bigger stakes involved than sitting on any one competitor or group of competitors at this stage. If a top skipper appears to be covering early in the race it is coincidental: he is staying on the same tack with the other boats only because it fits into his predetermined overall strategy of the day to do so. The first windward leg is the time to "get her going," to concentrate on sailing, and above all to go in the right direction. Your aim is to arrive at the first mark with a comfortable lead on the whole fleet. You may not succeed in this high goal; but you are substantially reducing your chances if you bother with covering. You might be able to get there a length ahead of your dearest rival by sticking to him like a Decal; but if you do, you will probably have to use binoculars to see the boat that is leading the race.

A race in which covering sometimes cannot be successfully accomplished even near the finish is the northwester which we discussed at some length in the last chapter. We emphasized how important it is to sail your own race on a northwest day.

If you are busy covering somebody you are presenting a third boat with the opportunity of sailing his own race while you cannot. On the second windward leg of a three lap course in the 1956 Jersey Coast Challenge series on Barnegat Bay I made exactly this mistake in an extremely shifty northwester. In an astonishingly short space of time our hard won lead had evaporated and two other boats had gone through us. To drive home the lesson, before we had gathered our scattered wits the boat we were trying to cover played a shift properly and in two quick tacks she had passed us too, leaving the *Flame* a badly shaken fourth. By revising our tactics and returning to tacking on headers with no regard for the rest of the competition, we managed to sneak back up to second the third time upwind. But we never could catch the number one boat, which trounced us by nearly half a leg of the course. It was Howard Lippincott in *Circus;* and it was small consolation when he went on to win the North American Championship of the class a few weeks later in the same kind of weather by using just such masterly tactics against 48 of the country's finest.

It is a great pity that the wind is invisible. If only we could put on some magic spectacles which would allow us to see the wind, how easy it would be to learn exactly how it operates. Lacking any such device, we can guess what the wind is doing only by observing its effect on other objects—mostly sailboats. We know quite a lot about what the wind does to the fleet. We know almost nothing about what the fleet does to the wind.

The wind is a fragile thing. It blows along the path of least resistance, like anything else that follows the laws of nature. Wind is much more easily deflected than a heavier fluid, like water. The result is that it is *far from homogeneous.* We are too prone to think of wind as a uniform steadily moving mass of air. Actually it is nothing like that. If we could see the wind, I am sure we would be amazed to observe how turbulent it is, how unsteady, non-uniform, full of holes and gaps and eddies and flaws.

Ralph M. Monroe, in "An Accomplishment of Sail," * describes the conditions in the lee of a lighthouse which consisted only of a skeletal steel framework projecting from some pilings on a shoal in the open sea. The sea was "in a rage." But "there was a back draft from the superstructure of the light tower as well as from the piling and its braces below. Being so broken up by this more or less open structure, the wind pressure apparently became more equalized than if the obstruction had been monolithic."

The greatest engineering catastrophe of the 19th century was the collapse of a new railroad bridge across the Firth of Tay in a strong gale one night in December of 1879. The bridge was actually blown down, partly because the designer had thought that its malleable iron lattice girders offered little resistance to the wind. The whole incredible tale is skillfully told by John Prebble in DISASTER AT DUNDEE, (Harcourt Brace & Co., 1957).

Everyone has at one time or another found himself becalmed in the lee of a wall of racing sailboats. What is not so well understood is that the "wall" can be full of holes, like the trestlework of the lighthouse or the bridge, and still raise hell with the air. One boat directly to windward of you is bad, but you may be able to cope with it; three or four boats scattered around up ahead may be disastrous. A bunch of boats widely separated and relatively far away can be exceedingly damaging to your wind. The lines of flow, broken up as they try to pass through and around the fleet, take longer to re-form than is generally recognized. It is interesting to note that the ice boat people report that they feel the harmful effects of backwind 200 to 300 feet astern of a competitor on the wind, with sails of only 75

* ON AND OFF SOUNDINGS, D. Van Nostrand Co., Princeton, 1951, p. 172.

square feet on an 18-foot mast. This is a far cry from the four or five mast lengths usually considered to be the extent of the wind shadow. The explanation lies in the high speeds maintained by these craft: velocities of 20 to 30 knots *to windward* are commonplace.

Now we see why the air goes dead around a starting area (Chapter 4). The boats milling about for an hour or so before the start play such havoc with the air stream that it has no chance to re-form. The wind blows around and up over any such area of turbulence and interference, tending to form new lines of flow which bend around the area, the stagnant air itself becoming a cushion which forms a part of and increases the size of the barrier. Thus the flow of air in the starting area becomes continually weaker as the afternoon progresses, unless the wind is so strong that it can blow away the whole stagnant air-mass, despite all the sails which are trying to hold it there like pins in a pin-cushion.

This explains why blanketing is so much more effective right after the start than later in the race. You must have noticed how easy it is to start almost even with another boat and yet find yourself 50 yards astern inside of two minutes. Had this happened out on the course you would not have fallen behind in any such spectacular fashion. The trouble at the start was that your competitor managed to edge into the undisturbed air and left you wallowing in the dead stuff; and your predicament quickly worsened as the mass of other boats continued to affect you adversely while he sailed away in the clear. This same phenomenon gives us an insight into why the second best starter is so seldom the boat alongside the best starter. A boat in another location entirely has a far better chance.

The air is badly cut up around the starting area for the obvious reason that that is where a lot of boats have been congregating. After the start, presuming that the first leg is to weather, the fleet splits apart laterally, and, even more important, moves to windward into fresh untrammelled air. When do the boats next come together again? At the first mark, of course. And not only is there a crowd there: it stays there temporarily. The procession to the second mark is a very effective wall, perhaps extending through a part of the diamond-shaped area used for the windward leg, perhaps near one of its edges (Fig. 11). No wonder the air tends to go bad at the first mark. How often have you complained, "When we went about we could fetch the mark; but we were headed as we neared it, and had to take two more hitches, which ruined us." You were not really headed. In fact, the fellows on the other tack probably thought that they were being headed at the same moment—an impossibility. What really happened was that *all* the boats approaching the mark sailed into such bad air that nobody could maintain his original course. The obvious moral is to allow more than you think you need for that last hitch on a light day.

We can learn another lesson from Figure 11. The air is subject to disturbance everywhere within the diamond and especially near points *A* and *B*. But it is worst affected on and near a direct line from *A* to *B,* because that is where, on the average, more boats are cutting up the air. Therefore on a light day one should do just what the authorities advise not doing: approach the mark near the edge or even outside the edge of the diamond, along one of the so-called lay lines. You simply cannot risk going up the middle. If you go up one side, the boats on the other side may beat you to the mark; but if go up the middle, boats on *both* sides will beat you, because there is more good air on either side than in the middle. It is your problem to decide ahead of time which side to prefer, from experience in the locality or your prognosis of the weather or whatever; then take the plunge when the time comes. You may explore the central regions in the middle of a long windward leg; but at the beginning and end of the leg, go off to one side and stay there.

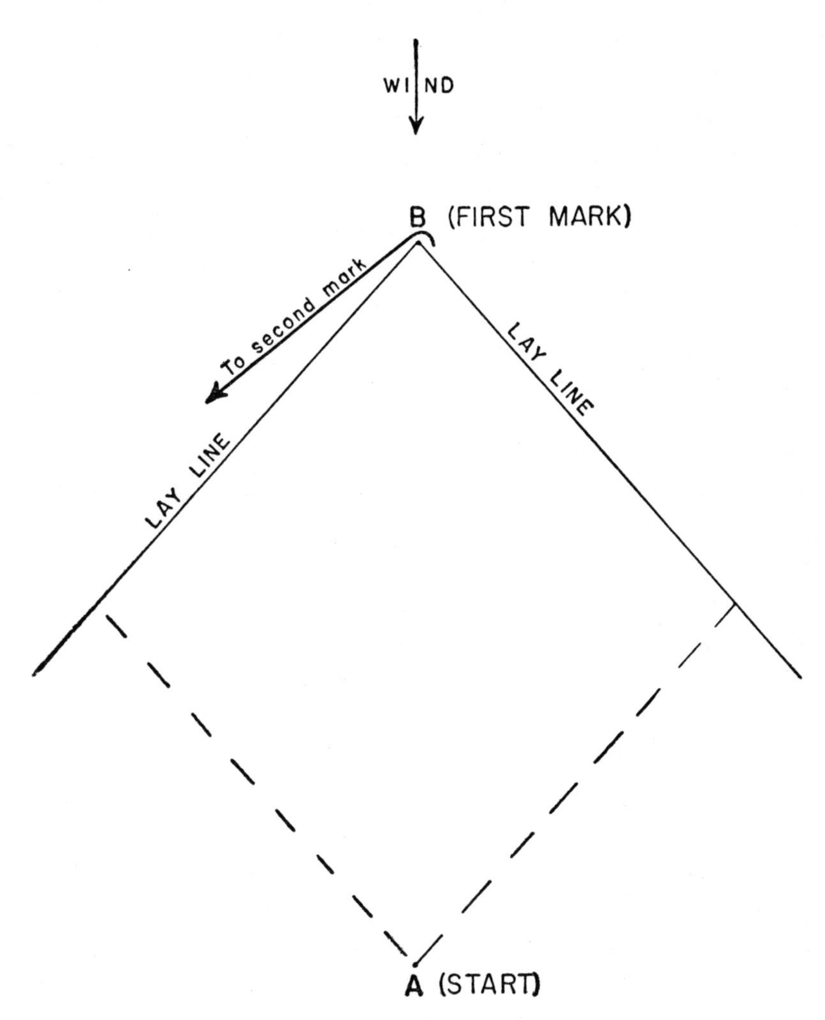

Figure 11. The diamond covers the area available for use in beating from *A* to *B*.

If the wind gets the staggers at a windward mark, it falls flat on its face at a windward finish. Here you have all the problems of the windward mark, plus boats hanging around after the race is over to watch the others finish, plus the committee boat itself, plus the spectator fleet. If the race is of the type popular nowadays in which the start and finish are the same line set in the middle of a windward leg of a triangle, it may be that the wind at the finish line has never recovered from the beating it took at the start. Frequently one sees the boats that approach the finish line "up the middle" of the last leg get passed a few yards from the end of the race by boats romping in on either lay line with a hard full.

How does all this affect covering? It can create a very knotty problem at the finish. The end of the race is the one time when you are definitely supposed to cover your nearest competitor. What if it is a light day in a big regatta and he elects to go up the middle? The danger signals are all flying: you should seriously consider throwing the text books overboard and going to one side. This is especially true if you are not the first class finishing. It is the big multi-class regattas with scores or even hundreds of boats finishing on the same line that really wreck the wind.

Do spectator boats do much harm? They annoy me very much, but not for the reason that most people think is important. You hear the irate skippers yelling "Slow down!" at the passing power boats. Of course the man with a couple of hundred horsepower banging away six feet from his ear couldn't hear Gabriel's trumpet being blown on his own foredeck; and he takes the shaking fist for a friendly wave, and waves back. Anyhow, the reason the skippers shout about slowing down is in the hope of decreasing the wake. I don't care so much about the wake: in most cases I'd rather have a nearby motor boat not slow down, but maintain course and speed and just go away. If he slows down he will only be in the vicinity that much longer. A large power boat may expose more area to the wind than a sailboat in your race; and a power boat's superstructure is so aerodynamically rough that it may well chew up the air more than a sailboat. The worst offenders are the spectator boats that sometimes "follow" a race. It wouldn't be so bad if they did follow; but as you approach the windward mark the spectator fleet must needs get there first and line up in a great wall just where they do you the most harm by aggravating the already poor situation at the top of the diamond. The only saving grace is that the damage is done impartially, hurting everybody in the race to about the same extent. When you see this condition developing, allow for it by overstanding slightly and then barrel in along the lay line with a rap full.

Do not be too willing to get yourself into the so-called safe leeward position. It is often a very unsafe leeward position. As you, on the port tack, approach a competitor on starboard and it becomes evident that you are not going to clear him, it is tempting to tack under his lee bow. Beware of accepting this gambit. Remember that as soon as you do this you are abandoning your own master plan, ceasing to sail your own race and beginning to sail someone else's. You were on port tack for some good reason; (well, there *should* have been a good reason). Now you are no longer on the tack of your choice. It is possible that by tacking for the enemy you are playing into his hand: he now tacks away, and you have split again but your relative positions are reversed and he is on your former tack. Even if he does not split, and you now both hold the starboard tack for a while, you are not going where you originally intended, and someone else in the fleet is going there. What's more, you are balked from tacking back to port by the boat on your weather quarter—which *you* chose to put there.

Don't be ashamed to bear off and cross under the other fellow's stern. If you were on a collision course anyway, you are losing only about a length by bearing away to clear him. Are you so sure you can go about without losing one length? By crossing under him you get rid of him much more effectively than by tacking under his bow. He is now no longer in your hair; and if he chooses to tack *after* you have crossed under him, (which they usually do), you are now on his lee bow, a sound place to be when both boats are on port tack.

The worst feature of the lee-bow position when both boats are on starboard tack is that you are frozen there. You can't tack away, even if several lengths separate the two boats. You can be forced off the course this way by a windward boat that does not tack for the mark when she ought to. Never assume that your opponent knows where the weather mark is:

"Sat. May 22, 1954, Larchmont. Started in a driving rain squall with puffs up to 35 out of the NW. Slogged along trying to stay in one piece, and all went well for a few minutes until we began to approach the lay line. With P - - - C - - - on our weather quarter, it was impossible to go about, although it soon became obvious to the veriest dunce that we could lay the mark. Finally shouted him about by telling him where it was. Should of course have born off instead to get some room, and then gone about under his stern. Overstood horribly, along with all of our bunch."

There is a curious phenomenon, which I do not pretend to understand, that can render the safe leeward position suddenly unsafe. If the windward boat is being sailed just the slightest bit too wide, it is impossible for the leeward boat to consolidate an apparently safe leeward position. Instead the two hang there, sailing side by side indefinitely, the frustrated skipper of the leeward boat unable to do anything about it. Evidently both boats must be strapped down absolutely as far as they will go and clawing to windward hammer-and-tongs before the safe leeward will operate the way it is supposed to. The minute the weather boat bears off only a trifle, the airflow patterns change in some way which requires the leeward boat to be *considerably* farther ahead before she can escape the blanket. A boat that is being sailed too wide is probably being sailed badly, and so you hope not to meet her in the middle of the race; but you may not be able to avoid starting alongside her, and it is just after the start that you are usually busy trying to pull out ahead of the boat close aboard your weather quarter.

CHAPTER 7

Series Strategy

Having just finished telling you to sail your own race, I am now in the somewhat embarrassing position of having to qualify that advice. If every race were a single isolated event not connected with any other race, the thoughts of the last chapter could stand unmodified. But hardly any of the races you sail are individual events. They are nearly always part of a series, and you are far more interested in doing well in the series than in doing well in any one race of the series. A daily first may be spectacular and it may catapult your name into the headlines; but it doesn't help you much if the next day you hit the skids. You will decline into oblivion as fast as you soared into prominence, while the man who, disregarding the newspapers but not the point score, plugs along with steady seconds and thirds and fourths ultimately wins the series. He is also recognized by the racing fraternity as the best sailor, even if he never won a race in the series; and this is as it should be, although the reporters and the publicity seekers may not agree.

In order to win series you sometimes have to stop sailing your own race and give a thought to the rest of the competition —but only near the end of the series. It is a major error to try to spot the probable leaders and direct your strategy against them early in the series. Too many things can happen, and there are too many potential winners, to consider selective tactics until the score has reached an advanced stage. I would go so far as to say that in a five race series you should seldom consider the point score before the fifth race and never before the fourth; and that in a three race event you should not do so until the last round of the last race.

It is wise to at least be aware of the approximate point score going into the next to last race, and you should know it cold before the last race. Many tactical decisions near the end of the series depend on it. From a number of interesting scoring situations in my records I choose one in which the point score played a deciding role during the last two days of a five day race week. After various haps and mishaps we entered the fourth race down five points on the leader, whom I shall call Smith, and five points ahead of the third boat, Jones. A ten point spread among the three leaders after only three races reflects the kind of weather we were (not) enjoying; but worse was to come. The fourth race:

"Started in a light SE on the first decent line of the week, and settled down on the long beat to windward. Smith stuck as close to us as he could, and we elected to go E, although it looked like a shift to S if anywhere. There was no point in trying to win the race with Smith second, even assuming we could stay ahead of him. Rather we wanted to let the others get the new wind first and then see what happened in the ensuing shakeup." There follow some remarks about sails, trim, etc. Then:

"It happened, all right. SW came in, we finished 13th, *nineteen minutes* behind the winner; Smith was 16th, Jones 7th. This puts Smith 2 points ahead of us, Jones 1. All depends on the last race now."

Next day: "Covered Smith up the weather leg, again a long one, hoping that some boats might get in between if we could slow him down enough. . . . We were third approaching the windward mark and, miraculously enough, three good boats were stacked in between us and Smith although we needed only two. On the reaches to the finish Smith could catch only one of them, which wasn't enough, and we won the series by one point." It doesn't say where Jones finished the last race, so I assume that he was somewhere down the drain.

Had we headed south in the fourth race it is pretty certain that we could have done much better in that race—and lost the series. Of course we would not have lost the series if Smith, who surely would have gone south with us, had not been able to stick next to us. We had reason to believe that if we both got into a strong steady breeze together he would do so; and I still defend our strategy, even though it had to be done as early as the fourth race. Smith later told us that he wanted to go south all the time, but didn't dare abandon us. Perhaps he, for his part, should *not* have tried to cover his series lead in the fourth race. That's hard to say from this distance; no one knew for sure that the southwester was coming, and he would have felt pretty silly going south if we had come out ahead by going east. It had been a week of just such peculiar happenings.

In the fifth race an unusual strategic situation developed suddenly at the weather mark. We approached it not very far ahead of Smith, and we were most gratified (and of course exceedingly lucky) when three boats from the other tack dropped neatly in between us. At this point I nearly made the bad mistake of switching my cover; that is, letting Smith go and camping instead on the nearest boat, which was very close to us indeed. This might have been the normal tactic, but to do so now could have been fatal, as I realized in the nick of time. It would have precipitated a spirited tacking duel between us and the next boat, and one of the others, or even Smith, might have passed us both. So instead of covering we gave the others free air to continue unmolested to the mark, gambling that we would all round in the same relative positions, which we did.

One of the most thrilling finishes of *Flame's* career depended for its punch on the score. This time the situation was not of our own making: it just happened. We entered the last race of the 1954 Miller Memorial Series for the championship of the Chesapeake in a 30-boat fleet with the score as follows on the place-point basis: *Vega* 5, *Scotch Mist* 7, *White Shadow* 7, *Flame* 8, *Boomerang* 9. Star men will recognize the boat names. To be three points out of first in competition of this calibre with only one race left was not encouraging. The last race was sailed over a three-times-around course in a westerly that kept increasing on each lap. We happened to find the first mark first, and consequently rounded ahead of those who overstood it, with a small lead on the fleet. On the second round *Flower* passed us, for the simple reason that we couldn't stop her. Near the end of the third windward leg *Boomerang* got into high gear and closed very fast, but we held second. On the final run home, the order was *Flower, Flame, Boomerang, Circus, Vega.* By this time it was blowing so hard that I doubt if I knew what the exact positions were, and certainly couldn't do anything about them anyway. Had we all finished this way, *Flame* and *Vega* would have been tied on points, but she would have beaten us in two out of the three races to break the tie in her favor. We were resigned to an honorable runner-up position, because there seemed not a chance in the world that anything could put another boat between ourselves and *Vega.* She was far ahead of the sixth boat, and *Flower* was increasing her lead ahead of us. But no series is over until the last finish line is crossed. A hundred yards from the finish a mammoth puff dismasted *Flower.* (See page 53.) It was a dead run, and she was able to drift across the finish line; but she finished between us and *Vega!* Meanwhile *Boomerang* was coming like a train of cars and succeeded in blanketing us just as we reached the committee boat. Had she beaten us, we would have been back in second place in the race, where we belonged, but now *third* in the series in the triple tie with *Vega* and *Boomerang.* But *Flame* got the nod in a photo finish (the committee said by six inches) to win the race and the series, for the first and only time in four attempts at the Miller Trophy.

When leading at the end of a series your tactics should become ever more conservative. You have nothing more to gain and everything to lose by taking chances now. Play it safe, protect your point lead, be content with an average start and a mediocre but respectable finish if you want to win the series. I learned this the hard way a few years ago by means of a recall. "There was a strong tide, which we were aware of, but it helped push us over too soon. We could not hear any numbers being called, and kept going much too long. By the time we had made sure that we were supposed to come back, and had done so, we re-crossed four minutes late! After almost reaching all the way around the very lop-sided course we finished 6th, with T. 2nd, to lose the series to him by one point. As usual, it was due to a bad combination of circumstances: the race committee's electric loud speaker was on the fritz; a very long line with the marker end favored created a bad jam there and at the same time put us so far away that we could not hear the numbers being called; the shape of the course, with no true windward leg, tricked us into thinking it was mandatory to stake everything on a hair-raising first start; by the same token we couldn't make up a four minute loss, which in turn was occasioned by the strong current which made a dead-run return to re-start exceedingly slow." Despite all these excuses the whole performance was a shabby one: we never should have taken any such chances with a three point series lead.

It becomes necessary to strike a happy medium between taking too many chances and not taking enough; between fouling out, and being so cautious that you give away points. Don't get yourself into inextricable jams; but on the other hand don't be so kind to your opponents that you hand them something they don't deserve. In the 1953 McNulty Series at Milwaukee we gave away a point by being conservative. *Flame* approached the last leeward mark of the last race, with one short reach to the finish line remaining, in fifth place. It was obvious that the order was not going to change on that reach. Dick Stearns was in first place, which was enough to give him the series by two points over us if we finished fifth. Just ahead of us, and outside us as we approached that mark, was a boat on which I was not sure we had an overlap. She was so far abeam that it was hard to tell, and it turned out afterward that her skipper was keeping her there because he thought we did have an overlap and he intended to allow us plenty of room. I had ample time to consider the situation and decided that there was no earthly use in trying to force an overlap. Even if we were entitled to one, which would certainly allow us to finish fourth, it would not improve our series position: we would still be second, by one point instead of two. Series second looked pretty good, and I wanted to protect it by running no risk of fouling out. At the last moment it became evident to the other skipper that I was not going to try for an overlap, and he crossed our bow with a surprised shout of "Thank you!" and of course beat us home.

So far so good; we went ashore and congratulated Dick. But imagine the jolt we received when he said, "Second by one point isn't so bad either." *One* point? Yes indeed: the boat that crossed the finish line second was disqualified for not heeding a recall at the start, an incident about which we knew nothing! That moved *Flame's* finish position up from fifth to fourth. And if we had not been so generous, and had pressed our inside position we could have finished third, and . . . and . . . ? A frenzied calculation revealed that in that case Stearns would have beaten us anyway on the two-to-one tie breaking rule, which was fortunate. If it had been the other way around, one Star skipper would have been seen kicking himself into Lake Michigan. This is doubtless hard to do, but I am sure I would have figured out how to do it, and that right quickly.

It is certainly a good general policy to press every advantage in a tight series, especially during the early races. If you lose the series by one point, you may feel that you lost that one point in the last race. Not at all: you could have picked it up just as well anywhere in the series in a dozen different places. The points lost the first day are just as costly, although perhaps not so heart-breaking, as those lost on the last.

CHAPTER 8

Crewing

What makes a good crew? * For one thing the skipper does. A crew is only as good as his skipper. It is not only poor taste but also an admission of your own weakness to blame your crew for losing a race. If ever a skipper grumbles about his crew, it is the skipper's fault. No one has to ship a poor crew. If your crew isn't performing well, it's because you haven't trained him properly; and if he is untrainable, you should have left him on the beach long ago.

The four parts of the yacht racing unit are the boat, the sails, the skipper and the crew. Without any one of them the team is helpless. It is evident that the two human parts of the team must be able to work in close harmony. The skipper-crew relationship is such a vital factor in winning races that you should be willing to devote at least as much thought and effort toward obtaining the best available crew as you do toward getting the best available sails. Let us look at some of the specifications of a good crew. They are not so very difficult to fill.

In selecting a crew, a skipper should look for someone possessing two qualities: a high sense of competition and a high I.Q. All the rest can be taught. On some boats the additional qualification of physical agility is a tremendous asset, but even that can be developed.

A crew must be all fired-up about every race. He must be out there first to win, and second to have a good time. This is another way of saying that his idea of having a good time is

* Although we shall continue to refer to "the crew" as a one man outfit, most of the ideas of this chapter apply equally to two, three or four man crews.

winning—not enjoying the scenery or beer-drinking on the downwind leg. As a skipper I have sometimes raced for an hour before suddenly becoming aware of the fact that I am in the middle of a magnificent picture of white sails and flying spray and blue sky and sea. If a crew can become as absorbed in the race as that, he is a good crew.

His intelligence is equally important. Try to get a crew who is at least as smart as you are. Otherwise he will be slow to learn, you will have to repeat instructions endlessly, and ultimately you will become his constant crutch. Sensing his inferiority, he will crawl into his shell and never be of any real help in the conduct of the race. You may eventually train a stupid crew to be mechanically adequate, but you want much more than that. In your quest for the best, do not settle for mediocrity.

You may wonder why I have not added a third requirement: that the crew have had some experience. Of course I hope he has had *some* kind of sailing background, enough at least to know what the words mean. I have never tried to train a bird-watcher who did not know what a halyard was, or which end was the bow. Such a procedure would be possible, but hard on the nerves. But the situation seldom arises, because most of the young fellows hanging around the clubhouse on race days and looking longingly at the boats making sail are water-rats from way back, and have lived most of their lives in and around boats. I assume that you will start with one of these, and not with your brother-in-law from Montana. The Montanan might end up just as good a crew, but it would take more time and patience than you have at your disposal.

It is a safe guess, however, that your new crew is fairly green at sailing in your class. It is only fair to him to take him out at least once before the first race to familiarize himself with the boat. If you can possibly take him sailing even before inviting him to race with you, that is 100% better. Then you can each take the measure of the other and decide whether it's a good idea. Somehow I never seem to be able to arrange this, with the result that I frequently find myself crossing the starting line with someone who has never been in the boat before. This procedure is not recommended.

Start with the bare essentials. Show him a few of the simplest things he has to do and let him practice each. If he asks for whys and wherefores, give him the basic reasons, but let the fancy refinements go until later. If he is as smart as you hope he is, he will see the reasons without asking. As soon as he has mastered a technique, make it plain to him that you are henceforth relying on him to take care of that point: it's in his department and he is responsible. For example, I have become so accustomed to having my crew read the time to me at the start that I cannot start any other way. This means that this important function is handled by every crew, however inexperienced. It is obvious to the veriest novice that timing the start is vital. He can tell by my preoccupation with other things that I am not keeping track of the time, and that if he couldn't give it to me when I needed it, we'd be lost. He is the timer and he knows it. He counts the seconds tersely down to zero, and when he says "GUN," by God it goes off. If it doesn't, I swear at the regatta committee, not the crew. They are more likely to be two seconds off than he is.

As the crew improves during the season, he should be willing and able to take on an increasing load of responsibility. This business of exactly who is responsible for what should be clearly delineated at all times. Skippers of big boats with several in crew find it helpful to write it all down in the form of station bills. I doubt if written station bills are necessary on small boats; but mental ones are. Each person must know what jobs he has to do. If you delegate a responsibility, stick to it. If the crew customarily puts the battens into the mainsail, do not insult his intelligence by asking him whether he has done so. If he says the sail is ready, hoist it; and then if the battens are not in, he will never forget them again—not on my boat, anyway. Of course there may be things which he does that you should check; but make it clear that this is a routine safety measure, and that you are not checking up on him. If you feel that you have to check up on him, do it surreptitiously; and if he lets you down too often, fire him.

Your crew is a human being: treat him like one. There are times when you must demand a great deal from him. Try not to demand the impossible. Spare him, so that he has to "give his all" only in emergencies, not all day long. Don't be a Captain Bligh. You are not running a picnic; but neither are you running a slave ship.

Compliment your crew rarely but sincerely. Once during a race is often enough to say "Nice tack"; or "Good work, that saved us the overlap." And say it when his superlative spinnaker handling really did save the overlap, and he was hoping that it would. Then he will come back happily for at least two more weekends. Meanwhile you will be watching for chances to say some more nice things, and soon he will be admitting—not in your hearing, of course—that you are a pretty good guy to crew with. One sincere compliment per week goes a lot farther than streams of them which gush so freely that they lose all meaning.

Let your crew sail the boat as often as you can, to and from races. It is a lot to ask, but let him skipper for a whole race if possible. This is the best reward a crew can get. If it is his introduction to skippering, it may mean that you will lose him the following year, because he'll be so enamored that he'll get a boat of his own. But after all, that's part of the game. You can lose your crew resignedly if it is because he has become so good that he wants to skipper. What more could you ask? It means that your one man school has been a success: someone has graduated. You can always recruit a new candidate.

Even though you are an experienced skipper, or perhaps *because* you are one, you may find yourself crewing sometimes, and if it is an important race or series you should feel honored to have been invited. When this happens, remember that you are for the nonce only a crew, definitely number two (or lower) on the boat. There should be no prima donnas aboard; but if there is one, he must be the skipper. And as Number Two, it is your job to supplement the skipper, to fill in where he needs you the most. There is not time, when a team is made up suddenly for just one series, to get to know your man as well as you should; but still you can be a good team if you work at it. If he is a crack tiller and sail handler, forget about the boat and concentrate on tactics for him. Soon he will be relying on you to do a lot of his thinking for him, and the boat will go all the faster. If you are all thumbs the minute you get a pair of pliers in your hands, tell him so. Then when something goes adrift he will not waste valuable seconds swearing at your clumsiness, but will immediately give you the tiller while he repairs the damage. If on the other hand you are mechanically inclined and he is not, tell him to sail the boat, you'll keep her in one piece. A good skipper is nearly always a first rate crew because he knows what most of the problems will be ahead of time. Two skippers working together can make a red-hot team.

If you think something is wrong with the boat or sails, be tactful in getting your idea across. It is almost impossible not to offend the skipper if you suggest that there is something he should be doing differently. The same applies to tactics. Heavy understatement sometimes does the trick. One good skipper of my acquaintance always sails with his wife as crew. He taught her how to sail, so that at first she could help him but little. Then as time went on she began making occasional contributions, such as "Do you think that might be the weather mark over there?" Somehow it always turned out to be the weather mark, just where she said it was; and suddenly he realized that that was only her polite way of saying, "Why don't you go about, knucklehead? We've been overstanding for the past two minutes." Now he listens most attentively to her suggestions—and they win many races.

Try to get in and stay in the skipper's mood. I was about to say, try to read his mind. The more you sail with him, the easier this becomes. The best crews need only a word from the skipper from time to time, no complicated instructions. Your top-drawer skipper in an important race is absorbed in sailing the boat, and what little attention remains goes into tactics and factors like wind and tide. He has none at all left over for the crew, who must shift for himself. The skipper cannot direct you during the race without taking his mind off something more important. If you can get the feel of the boat and sense what the skipper is trying to accomplish, he will be everlastingly grateful. If you pile out to windward without being told at the right moment when it breezes up, but know enough to stay below on just those occasions when it breezes only momentarily and is about to die down again, your skipper will bless you. Pretty soon you will learn to tack ship without a warning order. You will sense from the commotion aft, or from the skipper's glance abeam, or just from his expression, that he is preparing to go about, and you will be getting the jib off the cleat as he starts to put the tiller down.

Don't talk. Observe. Save your comments for occasions when they are really necessary. If you are standing slightly below a mark on a broad reach, the chances are that it is because the skipper wants to be down there, and with the mark in plain sight he sees it too. But if you are above a mark, it would be wise to tell him about it: it may be hidden from his view behind the sails. If he says "I know it," in a curt, annoyed tone, don't feel hurt. He can't help thinking that you are trying to tell him to bear off, and he may have his own good reasons for holding high. But it is worth the retort, because you have to know that he has seen the mark. When I am skippering I try to school myself to acknowledge all observations with thanks, even if I am sometimes a jump ahead of the crew and the information he is giving me is irritatingly stale. I don't want to discourage those observations: sometimes they contain vital news.

Adopting the skipper's frame of mind usually means keeping pretty quiet. I know of few skippers and no top-notch ones who are talkative. They are much too busy thinking to talk. I once crewed for a very fine skipper who is notoriously morose while racing. I decided that I could be just as glum as he could, and I don't think we exchanged two unnecessary words during the entire race. Almost needless to say, we won; and I think he considered me a satisfactory crew. The odd thing is that we both enjoyed the race.

A few years ago a young fellow in our club sold his International 110 and did not replace it with another boat. Instead he crewed with me for nearly two years. This was an unprecedented bit of good fortune for the *Flame*: to have a steady crew for two seasons who was already a skipper in his own right was indeed a windfall. We eventually became so used to each other that we were thinking pretty much as a unit. I did not realize how thoroughly I had learned to rely on him until it was pointed up by a relatively small incident in the middle of a crisis. We were approaching a weather mark, to be left to port, in a procession of boats on the starboard tack. As so often happens, we had cut it very fine and it looked as if we might not lay the mark. There were boats on our weather quarter—naturally. (Fig. 12.) With about 100 yards to go to the mark, too intent to take time out to look around, I asked Bill whether we could tack if we had to. He looked, hesitated, and said, "It would be close." I knew by his tone that he meant we damned well couldn't, and he knew I knew it. He was only softening the blow, because experience told him that that was the way to get the best results out of me. I settled down to sail the boat like mad, and we did just lay the mark.

All this was preliminary; now comes the point. As we rounded the mark and paid out sheets with a sigh of relief, Bill said quietly but very authoritatively, "Now we go onto the other jibe." Bill was not in the habit of delivering ultimatums on the *Flame*; this was the first time he had ever made such a positive statement, amounting to a tactical decision. But he said it so matter-of-factly, with such an air of knowing what he was talking about, that I jibed instantly, without even thinking of questioning him. He had recognized that, during the approach to the weather mark, as far as planning the next leg was concerned I might as well have been on Mars. He could see that he must temporarily take over the duties of the skipper, and he unhesitatingly did so without bothering to tell me about it. He surveyed the leeward leg, checked the location of the next mark, planned the jibe and executed it, incidentally permitting us to pass two boats. We didn't win that race; but we finished fourth, thanks to the smoothness of the whole maneuver at that mark, which gave us runner-up position in the series. I considered it the high point of Bill's crewing career. Needless to say, he now has his own boat again, and does very well with it. You can seldom keep them up in the sharp end of the boat when they are as good as that.*

* There are those who, for reasons of temperament and personality, are so constituted that they prefer crewing to skippering as a steady diet. This is a book for skippers; but for the benefit of any crewing enthusiasts who might be wandering through its pages, we quote a paragraph from Ian Proctor's RACING DINGHY HANDLING, (Robert Ross & Co., Ltd., Southampton, England) which devotes five chapters to the art of crewing.

"As already mentioned, there is no better way of learning to race your own

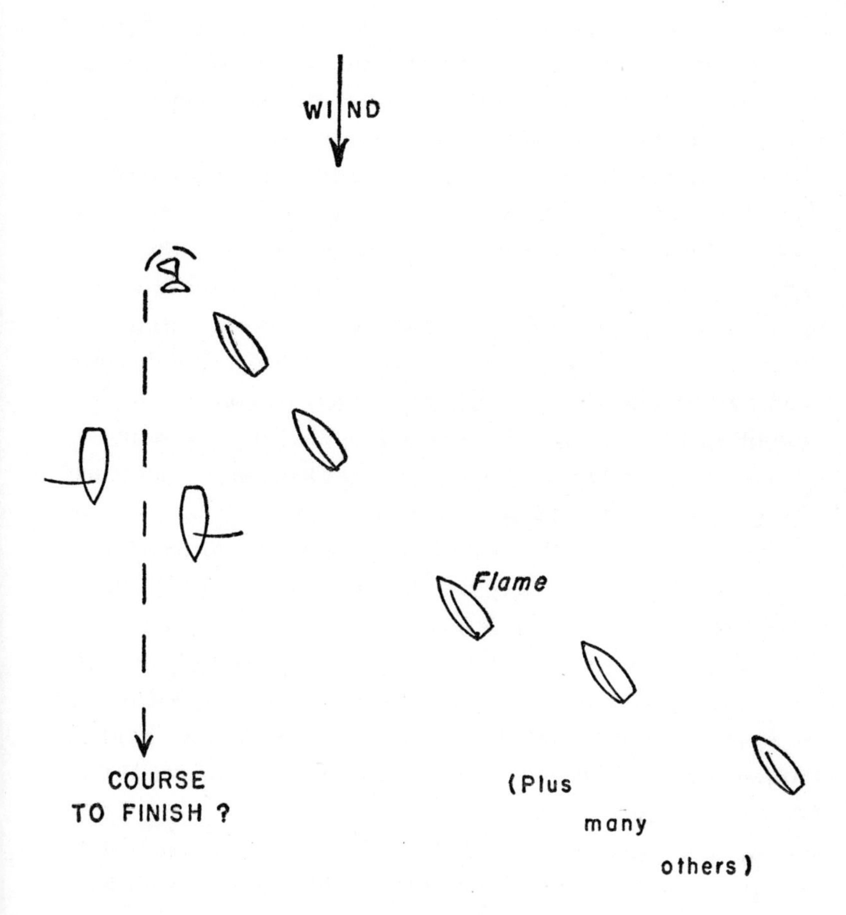

Figure 12. *Flame* is in a most unenviable position unless she can lay the mark.

Don't be too quickly discouraged if a green crew seems poor at first. Give him half a chance. Of course he will be a disappointment after the expert you have just lost. But if he is sufficiently enthusiastic, he ought to improve rapidly. Enthusiasm is the one ingredient without which no one can become a good crew—or a good skipper either, for that matter. A boy who had never been aboard a boat until four years ago became interested in sailing. Cajoled into it by a contemporary who races, he bought a wretched old Star for a song, reconditioned it and started learning from scratch: maintenance, small boat handling, racing rules, everything. I have seldom seen anyone so inept as he was as a beginner. I shouldn't have given him one chance in a hundred of staying with it. *Within three years* he had won a race, against top competition. Not long ago I had the pleasure of having him as crew in a weekend series. He was one of the smoothest performing crews I have ever had aboard. Every motion was automatic. At the end of the series I realized to my astonishment that I had never once snapped at him or even raised my voice during the entire weekend. That this could happen on *Flame* is extraordinary; to have it happen with someone who had never sailed with me before is unheard-of. That a complete landlubber could become so accomplished in so short a time should be a heartening thought to other beginners. If he could do it, anyone can.

---

boat than by crewing for a good helmsman, but crewing should not necessarily be regarded simply as a stepping-stone towards helming and skilful ownership. A really first-class crew is worth his weight in gold and is constantly sought after by helmsmen for big and important races; therefore, someone who specializes in this task and sets out to make himself a really top-line foresheet hand, may have the great satisfaction of crewing numbers of winning dinghies and may very well consider crewing as an end in itself and a job worthy of receiving his continued attention, rather than just a rung on the ladder to good helmsmanship."

Emil Mosbacher, Jr., one of the absolutely top ranking skippers in the U.S. today, and one of the most modest, is responsible for saying in jest what has more than a grain of truth in it for us all: "My crew spends the afternoon getting the boat out of the fixes that I get it into."

CHAPTER 9

Tides

Strictly speaking, tide refers to the rise and fall of water, and current refers to its horizontal motion. The word tide, however, is so generally used by yachtsmen in the sense of current that I shall not bother to differentiate between the two. It will be obvious, I trust, that if I say "The tide was against us," I do not mean that we were going straight down.

The importance of a tidal current depends mostly on its velocity, but also on the ratio of that velocity to the wind's velocity. A current of half a knot may decide the race on a very light day, and may perhaps be disregarded if it is blowing 20. If the tides are strong in a given locality, they may dictate the whole policy of the race. In much of the racing around the coast of England, for example, the proper calculating and exploiting of the tides is almost the only feature of the race that matters. Sir Fisher Dilke, in commenting on the fact that compasses are little used in British racing, remarked, "What for instance is the use, with the wind south-west, of knowing the bearing of the East Lepe buoy from somewhere between Egypt Point and Gurnard Ledge when there is a three-knot tide running eastward at the East Lepe and a one-knot bit of westerly tide still running where you are at the moment? None whatever. You go on for one more tack than you think you ought to, and then have a shot at it from a range of a mile and a half. When you get a mile from it you'll know without a compass whether you are going to fetch or not. And you generally are not. . . . The difference lies nearly entirely in our strong tides and narrow waters." * I think most Americans would pack up and go home if they were asked to race in a three-knot current at the East or any other Lepe.

There seems to be no satisfactory way of finding out ahead of time how to gauge the tides in unfamiliar waters. The available government tide and current charts are of such small scale that they give only the vague general outline of the behavior of the current, failing to provide the detail needed by the racing yachtsman. Past experience and local knowledge help. The only way to decide what to do in an unknown current is to observe what it is doing to you and to the other boats on the spot; and unfortunately it is then often too late. Hear Gerard Lambert on the subject; he is racing J-boats in England:

"In one race in the Solent I was badly beaten. On the run down wind I led the entire fleet, rounding the first buoy well in the lead. The wind was very light. As we came round the mark we hauled up for a windward leg of the course. To our amazement, instead of going forward we began to drift backward, the tide against us was so strong. We immediately dropped a kedge anchor and sat there waiting for the others to come along. Surely they would anchor alongside of us and when the wind was strong enough or the tide changed we could resume the race. Not at all!

"As each of the five boats reached the buoy they did not anchor nor did they head up into the wind. They continued blithely by me, waving a friendly hand as they went, and headed for the north shore, two miles away. We could see the tide carrying them away from the course, and wondered if they were crazy. But as they approached the shore the tide lessened, as it always does near shore, and they began slowly to make progress toward the finish line. Inch by inch they crept up along that shore and we sat there, at anchor. There was nothing for

* OBSERVER ON RANGER, Sir Fisher Dilke, Bt., Herbert Jenkins, Ltd., London, 1938.

us to do but wait for the wind. If we repeated their performance and went over to the shore we would be three miles behind them. We finished a miserable last. Unfortunately we never sailed that course again under those conditions, and had no opportunity to take advantage of what we had learned." *

The most thorough analysis of the effect of tidal current on a sailboat that I have seen is the chapter on the subject in Ted Wells' excellent book.** If you do not already own this book, get it. It is the most sprightly, most easily read, least pompous and most down-to-earth of all the racing books. If you can weed out the inaccuracies in the tide chapter (and there aren't many of them), the rest will tell you a lot that you didn't know, particularly if you are good at reading and interpreting diagrams.

One bit of misinformation which has been published often (including *loc.cit.*) is that currents run less swiftly over shoals and shallows than elsewhere. Just the opposite is the truth. The old proverb has it straight: still water runs deep. The reason is obvious enough. Think of the sound or bay as a pipe through which the water is flowing. A shoal is the equivalent of a narrowing of the pipe, so of course the water must flow faster there than in the wide (deep) places in order to maintain a uniform rate past all stations. This is worth noting when racing in a body of tidal water in which you are using government marks as turning buoys. These marks are usually placed on shoals, so that the current is always strongest right at the marks, exactly where you may desire it the least. If the current is adverse at such a mark, get away from it in the quickest possible fashion immediately after rounding, even if you have to go sideways to do so. The current may be substantially less 100 yards from the mark; get out of the current first, and square away on your course afterward. The direction and strength of the current

* Gerard B. Lambert, ALL OUT OF STEP, (Doubleday, 1956) p. 209.

** T. A. Wells, SCIENTIFIC SAILBOAT RACING, (Dodd, Mead & Co., New York, 1950), Chapter 8 of Part III.

at a mark are easily seen as the water races past the anchored buoy (See page 84).

It can easily happen that one leg of a race crosses the mouth of a bay or harbor, from the buoy marking the point on one side of the harbor to that marking the point on the other. If this harbor is a tributary of a larger bay or sound, the harbor itself may enjoy relatively still water while the current outside is moving across the mouth from one side to the other at a good clip. If you are running downwind from *A* to *B* (Fig. 13), with the tide against you, always favor Course 1; but if the tide is with you, take Course 2. On a long run in a light breeze it takes very little current to decide the race in favor of those who play it correctly.

I confess that my ignorance of the action of tides on a hull has been most profound. I have never paid enough attention to tides, and only recently a few drubbings have brought home the necessity of being more observant of this fascinating and little understood department of the race. I am glad to be able to report a race in which, for once, we noticed the tide in time to use it correctly; it was an eye opener.

We were beating out of Huntington Bay into Long Island Sound in a moderate northerly, with the harbor current negligible. Our weather mark was the big flasher off Eaton's. As most of the fleet approached it on starboard tack, *Flame,* which had been doing so-so, was a close fourth. We tacked short of the mark, to avoid going astern of the three leaders, and settled down on starboard tack approximately as shown in Figure 14. Suddenly about a quarter of a mile from the mark I said "Oh boy!" "What does that mean?" asked the crew, who knew that it certainly meant something, so few are the expressions of encouragement that emanate from my end of the boat during a race. I had noticed that although our bow was not pointing at the mark, and we looked as if we would fetch far to leeward of it, yet by pinching just the least bit above our normal course I

Rosenfeld

Current revealed by a buoy.

New York Times

"Unable or unwilling to jibe."

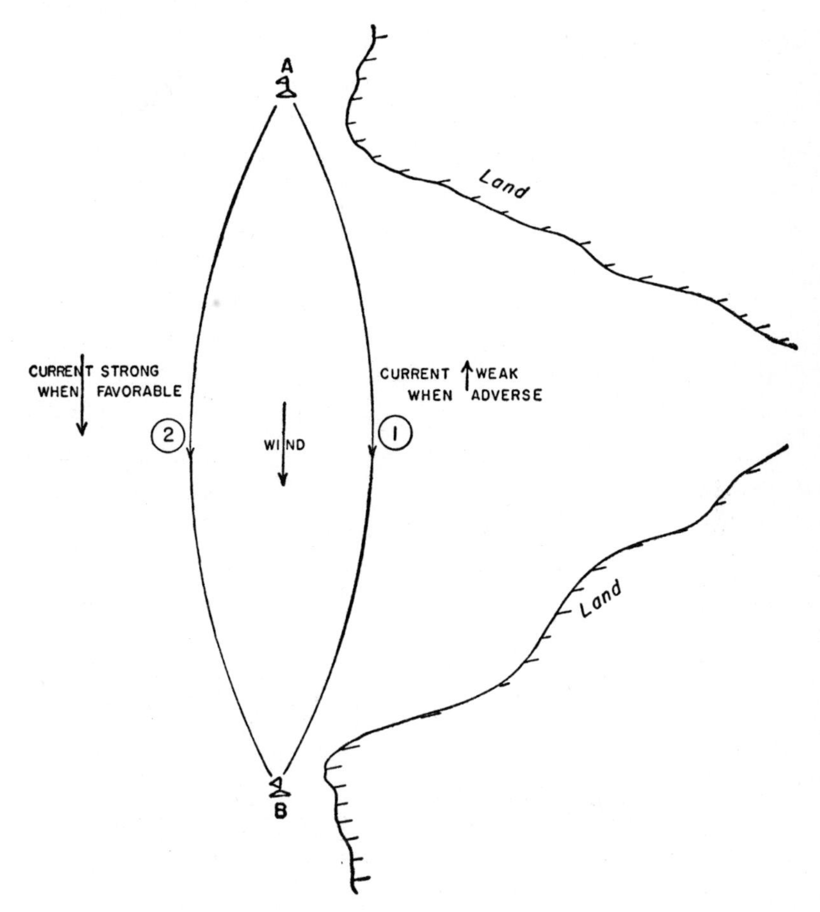

Figure 13. Choice of courses in a tideway.

could hold the mark stationary against the distant Connecticut shore. What a pleasant discovery! It meant that we could eat up to windward under the bows of the other three boats, which we proceeded to do in an astoundingly rapid fashion, and might even lay the mark without tacking. Well, we couldn't quite do that. But by the time we got there we were so far ahead—of boats which only a quarter-mile back had been leading us—that we tacked to port with never a worry about being able to cross them. A very short port hitch took us to the mark, and we maintained our stolen lead easily to the finish.

The interesting thing was that the other skippers did not guess what was happening. Although they surely saw us moving sideways to windward, they sturdily maintained their full and by courses. One of them, who must have started the last starboard hitch a good 75 yards abeam of us to weather, told me later that he missed the mark by eight feet and had to tack again. How easily he could have moved his boat eight feet to windward without tacking, if we moved ours nearly 75 yards to windward! What was happening of course was that the strong Sound ebb was dead against us; and that by altering course a hair to starboard we put it under *Flame's* lee bow, with the benefits described. It was the most striking example of a successful lee bow situation that I had ever seen. Doubtless those who race where there is always a strong current do much more spectacular things every day.

We close this brief discussion of tides with a problem which was propounded in Alfred F. Loomis' column in a recent issue of *Yachting* magazine. This is not a puzzle book and I promise not to inflict you with any more of these; but the problem has some merit in helping us to think clearly about the effects of a following current.

Joe challenges Pete to race a fixed distance downstream in a wide, deep river with a current which flows everywhere uniformly at ten knots. They have only one boat, so each has a

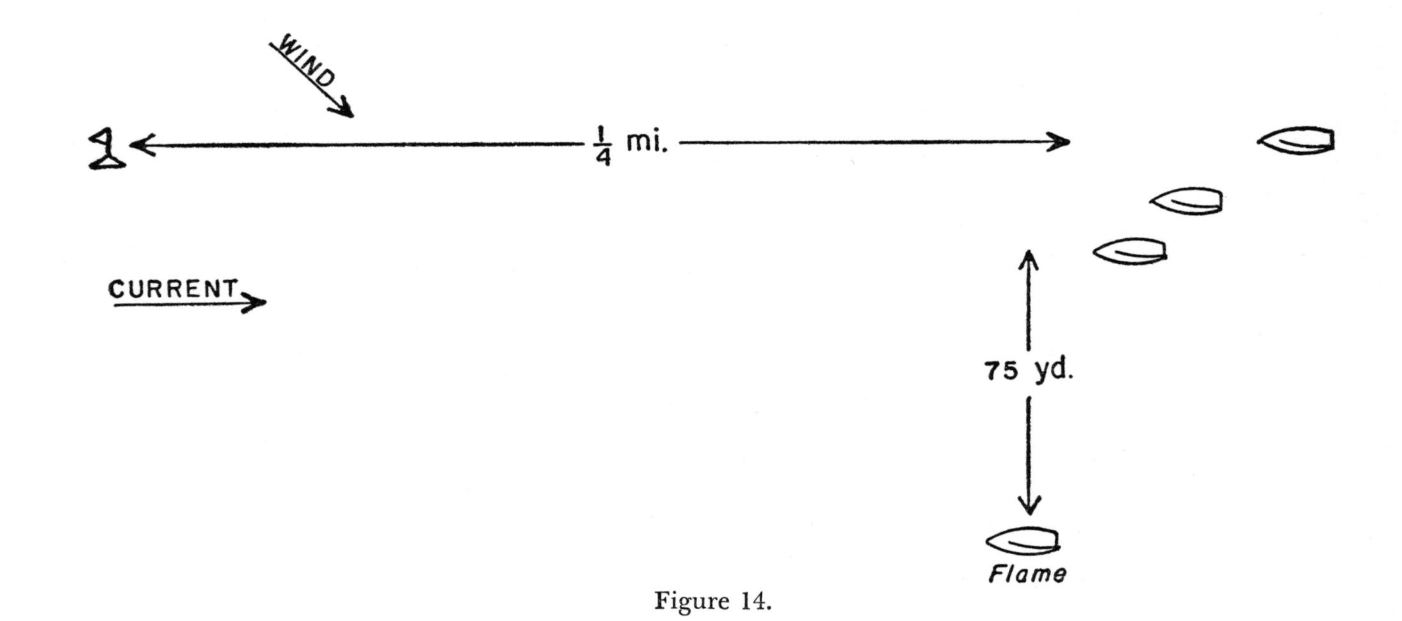

Figure 14.

try at it, carefully timed. For the sake of the problem, they are assumed to be skippers of equal ability. Joe makes his run on a day when he has a ten-knot following breeze; Pete chooses a day of flat calm. Who wins?

You guessed it: Pete wins. But why?

CHAPTER 10

The Weather

The good seaman sees everything alow and aloft; his eyes are roving all over the vessel, across the sea to starboard and port, and ahead and astern. He notes every vary of the cloud, every change of the swell, every shift of the wind. He catches and interprets the phases of ocean life. Not a bird moves over the wave, not a fish breaks the surface but his quick glance catches the glimmer of the wing or the glint of the fin. To him the sunrise and sunset speak, foretelling the weather; he reads the clouds and questions the drift and color of the horizon. His eye and hand play together in this fascinating game of voyaging, and the ship laughs her way onward, contented under the watchfulness of an observing master.

—Thomas Fleming Day

Several times in the earlier chapters I have been guilty of dropping casual remarks about the importance of playing the wind shifts, going to the west "if you expect it to shift into that quarter," and so on. You may have thought at the time, "That's all very well, but how are we supposed to know how the wind is going to shift? I notice he doesn't tell us that!" Of course not—because, sadly, he can't. But now he is going to stick his neck out and try.

There are many excellent books about the weather. I haven't read them. Most of them contain about nineteen chapters of theory and one of forecasting. Well, you have to know the theory to be a professional forecaster. But the trouble with these books for us is that yachtsmen don't want the kind of forecast that interests the rest of the population. The average householder, golfer or weekender wants to know whether it's going to rain. Now that synthetic sails are here to stay, the racing skipper couldn't care less whether it rains or not. Furthermore, before the start of a race you are not interested in knowing what it is going to do in the Mississippi Valley two days from now; you are vitally concerned with what it is going to do right here two hours from now. And you can't often get that kind of forecast: you have to roll your own.

Local short-range weather forecasting is probably the easiest kind there is. Surely there must be textbooks covering the subject, and courses of instruction. I considered looking it all up before starting this chapter, and then thought better of it. I might have picked up some of the technical jargon, which would only have confused you and probably me too. You are an amateur meteorologist and you can better understand me if I remain an amateur. So let the professional weather men laugh at our crude methods and our naive approach: we have no radiosondes, no humidity gauges, no up-to-the-minute weather maps aboard our racing craft. We shall have to make do without any instruments but our eyes and without any apparatus except what we carry in our heads.

To begin with, it will be a big help to you to understand the basic principles on which the weather operates. This much is in the books.* Those who know about the endless procession of highs and lows that cross the country, and have an inkling of the kinds of weather associated with them and with the "fronts," may skip the next few paragraphs. For those who don't I shall try to present the story as briefly as possible. We must get this behind us before we can talk intelligently about racing weather.

* Read, for instance, the weather section of Charles F. Chapman's famous PILOTING, SEAMANSHIP AND SMALL BOAT HANDLING, (Motor Boating, N.Y.). This treatment has the signal advantage of being written by a yachtsman for yachtsmen.

Basic principle No. 1 is that weather moves from west to east across the United States and in most other parts of the temperate zones, because of the rotation of the earth. This means exactly what it says: big chunks of weather move as units, and always in a general easterly direction. Benjamin Franklin is said to have been the first to notice this phenomenon. He discovered that the same storm which had departed from Philadelphia reached Boston a day or so later. In recent years our attention has been so frequently focussed on the progress of hurricanes that most people are familiar with the way these great storms travel. They move substantially from south to north, and thus are exceptions to the usual trend; except for that, their progress is just like the progress of any other storm.

Bad weather is associated with a low barometer. Essentially a low barometer marks an area perhaps hundreds of miles across and a thousand miles long where the air pressure is below normal. What makes these "lows" appear, and grow, and after a life of days or weeks finally dissipate, no one knows. Wherever a low exists, air (wind) tries to rush into it to fill up the partial vacuum. You might think that this would quickly happen, and that the pressure would immediately be equalized; but it isn't so simple as that, for various complicated reasons which needn't concern us. What does happen is that a big whirlpool forms in the atmosphere. In the case of a tropical hurricane the whirlpool is nearly circular, symmetrical and very well defined, and the winds whirling around its center blow with exceedingly high velocities. In a normal storm of the temperate zones, the whirlpool is weak or non-existent. Instead of a circular shape the barometric low may assume the form of a trough, down the middle of which runs a long line marking the region of lowest pressure. This line is called a front (actually not a line but a wall, because the atmosphere is three-dimensional); and it is along this line that one meets a change in the weather. The existence of fronts is a relatively recent meteorological discovery. The word has been in the vocabulary for about twenty-five years.

The simplest front is a cold front which extends in a north-south direction perhaps all the way from Canada to Mexico. To the immediate east of the front the weather is gloomy, windy and rainy, the barometric pressure is falling, and the wind blows from some easterly quarter (in an attempt to "fill" the low). To the immediate west of the front the wind is west or northwest, the skies are clearing, the barometer rises rapidly, and the temperature is much lower. As the front marches across the country from west to east it carries all this weather with it. For an observer stationed in a fixed locality the cycle proceeds somewhat as follows. Behind the previous front was an area of high barometric pressure which may have taken two or three days to pass. Gradually the northwest winds have died down. Now the temperature rises, the barometer falls, and the wind goes over to the south or southeast. A haze may form. Previously clear skies film over with light clouds until gradually the sun is obscured behind increasing cloudiness, and as the wind backs into the east or northeast, it rains. The low trough is at hand. Pretty soon (in a matter of hours or days) its passage is marked by a violent wind-shift to the west or northwest; the temperature drops ten degrees in as many minutes; the rain slacks and soon ceases; the clouds rise, changing from gray leaden layers to whiter fluffier masses which then break up and dissipate; and finally the barometer, which has been rapidly rising, is high again and the cycle is complete.

Weather forecasting would indeed be simple if this pattern were always followed. If all lows were the same "depth," a glance at the barometer would tell you how near the front was and you would know exactly when to expect the change-over to clearing weather. But the weather gods play a thousand variations on the basic theme, never coming up with exactly the same thing twice. Sometimes it is five days between lows, sometimes one day; the lows and fronts are not always well defined long straight lines—in fact they almost never are; lows can develop little secondary lows close beside them; fronts curl around and become "occluded"; and a hundred and one other variants occur to confound the forecaster. Despite all this, the steady progress from west to east does happen: *the weather always moves in from the west.* This fact, unrecognized by many people, is a cardinal principle of local weather forecasting.

It is perhaps natural, though incorrect, to look to windward for the new weather. Suppose it has been overcast for days and is raining on a very low barometer with the wind strong east—a typical nasty day. Up to windward, a mile or so away, you can see extra heavy rain falling from a more than usually black cloud. Is that rain going to reach you soon? It is not. But if a black cloud appears to *leeward,* in the west, I have news for you: you are going to be wetter before you are any drier. That black cloud will move up to you, *against* the wind, and dump its rain on you. What you have to visualize is that the whole enormous storm system, clouds, rain and wind, is moving majestically from west to east at 20, 30 or 40 miles per hour, no matter how the winds within it are blowing. You can tell at once who are the weather-minded people in the crowd by observing who looks to the west. If there is a perceptible brightening in that direction, there's hope for clearing soon; and when the sun breaks through in the west, the storm is over.

As has already been hinted, there are dozens of exceptions to the rules. One of the commonest might be worth mentioning because it applies to the New England coast, a popular yachting area. Some storms move up the east coast, behaving much more like baby hurricanes than like fronts. They cause the famous three-day northeasters with their associated rain. A storm of this kind moves parallel to the coast a few miles out to sea; and until it passes off to the northeast there is not much hope of clearing weather.

It should begin to be plain that anyone could predict pretty accurately the *general* weather picture if he had an up to date weather map in front of him. This is exactly what the professional meteorologist does have. He gets his barometric readings from all over the country by teletype or radio, and from these and other necessary data collected in the same way, he draws his map of lines of equal barometric pressure—the *isobars*. He thus has a beautifully clear picture of almost exactly what the weather is doing right now all over the country. Only two steps remain: (1) to decide what the map will look like in the near future, which means estimating how fast the lows and fronts will move and in what directions; and (2) to interpret the map and translate it into every-day weather words. There are traps and pitfalls surrounding both these steps; but in spite of the difficulties, the expert gets excellent results. The weather man takes a lot of ribbing; but, although you may not believe this until you start "keeping score" yourself, modern forecasting hits an extremely high batting average. The last figure I heard, some years ago, was that the official U.S. forecasts for 24 hours in advance are right 85% of the time. Methods are improving every year, and one suspects that the forecasts are correct on an average of at least 90% of the time today in most places.

You, of course, don't have hourly teletype readings or anything like that to tell you what the isobars are doing. But you do have, if you are not too isolated, a reasonably recent weather map. Most big cities have at least one daily newspaper which carries the map. To be sure, by the time it reaches your hands the map is already about twelve hours old. But by simply projecting the whole picture a few hundred miles eastward you can make an estimate of the situation at hand. This is where your own barometer comes in: it can help you to correct your estimated barometric surroundings. With the aid of the map and your known barometric pressure you can read approximately what the major trends may be in the next day or so. This is the first step in weather forecasting.

If you don't have a map, the barometer alone, judiciously consulted, can almost make up for it. It doesn't make much difference whether the barometer is high or low; whether it is rising or falling is what counts. The words "Stormy," "Fair," "Very Dry" and the like decorate the dials of some barometers. That's *all* they do. Disregard them. Tap the glass, and if the needle moves to the right the barometer is rising, to the left falling. You take it from there.

I said that this was only the first step. No one can learn to be a good weather man solely by reading maps and looking at instruments. All the rest is practice in coordinating your information with what you see going on around you. Many people, outdoor men like fishermen and woodsmen and others whose livelihood and even lives may depend on accurate weather forecasting, become experts without any instrumental aid at all. The old New England farmer or fisherman—and I say old with admiration and respect, because he isn't really good at the weather until he has had fifty or sixty years of practice—cannot tell you exactly how he does his forecasting. He peers at the sky, breathes the air, considers the temperature and the humidity, recalls what yesterday was like, and says, if he is in a talkative mood: "Feels as if it might come on to rain a bit this afternoon." Note the word "feels." A lot of your weather forecasting has to be done "by the feel of it." This feel, if you stop to analyze it, is a semi-conscious coordination and tabulation of all the other similar days in your mental filing cabinet. You know *from experience* what this day is going to be like.

If you wish to improve your weather forecasting ability (and what sailor doesn't?) you should acquire the habit of becoming attuned to the weather every day, not only on race days. A close acquaintanceship with the weather is an essential to good forecasting. To use the terminology of electronic machines, you build up a "memory bank" of information to be called on when you need it. The more weather you can observe, the more complete your storehouse of information. Being familiar with the day to day weather situation, summer and winter, carries an added psychological reward. You become calmer, less fretful about the weather as soon as you understand it well enough to follow its progress and anticipate its future course. Your forecasting is more effective when you can handle it as if you were dealing with an old and sympathetic friend instead of trying to outguess a hostile enemy.

How can weather forecasting be of direct help in sailing a race? In many ways. It goes without saying that if there is a front in the neighborhood you should know about it and be prepared to sail toward it. The fresh new northwester which accompanies a cold front would certainly decide any race. Or suppose a northerly has blown itself out and the barometer is stagnant high. From what direction should you expect a new wind? The position and proximity of the next low is a reasonably sure guide. If there is a strong, deep low not far away to your west, you may expect the counter-clockwise circulation around it to produce southerly winds in your vicinity. Again, if this low is very near or you are in it, look for thunderstorms.

But most of the time the situation is not clear-cut. The weather map may, in summer, consist of a few widely spaced isobars meandering in haphazard fashion across the whole country. Widely spaced weakly organized isobars mean a shallow gradient—a very slowly changing barometer. This in turn means light and variable airs. What wind there is in such a situation is usually local and possible thermal. Predictions are much more difficult and depend more than ever on local knowledge. If you can accurately predict the winds one hour ahead of time on a day like this you may consider yourself an expert.

It is on just such days that many summer races are sailed in the United States. The barometer and the map have been motionless for hours, maybe days. But there are other indications to be considered. The cloud formations may give you a clue; watch for the motion of distant smoke; is it hazy or clear, and what does that mean in your particular region? Is it hotter than yesterday, or cooler? Did it feel like this yesterday morning, and if so, what happened in the afternoon? Experience, memory, observation; these must be your guides.

There are on the market various weather predicting gadgets. They usually consist of a series of cardboard dials which you set to match the present barometer, temperature and wind direction and perhaps some other factors. You then turn to the pages of a booklet where the readings are coded into a forecast. Actually these gadgets are very good: they work. There is only one hitch. At the bottom of the list of various forecasts there is one code number marked "Unpredictable." Unfortunately when you code the conditions of a normal midsummer day into the machinery, it turns to "unpredictable." When the conditions are clear cut, the gadget makes a sound forecast; but under such conditions you can make the same forecast without the gadget. The days that baffle you baffle it also.

On the morning of every race day a considerable share of my attention is diverted—or I should say reserved—for weather observation. This is at least as important to me as getting the boat readv. While I am puttering around the boat, launching it or whatever, I am constantly watching the day and thinking about it. Sometimes I stop and stare out over the water for a minute or so; and if anyone interrupts my thoughts just then he is likely to get a very sharp retort. I don't even like to be asked about the weather itself, the very thing that is occupying me. "What's it going to do this afternoon?" Even after all my morning's musings I don't know. It doesn't work that way. The most you (or I or anyone else) can hope to do on a difficult and doubtful day is to open your mind to the possibilities; make yourself receptive to the hints; observe the clues, and store them away. Do your best to "get the feel of the day." Then when things begin to happen during the race, the pieces of the puzzle drop into place, the heretofore chaotic local picture takes on form and meaning, and you can select the one among all the possible half-formed forecasts you were mulling over which it is now clear fits the situation in the light of latest developments. If you did not have behind you the background of the morning's observations, plus the weather wisdom of all the rest of your life, you could not hope to do as well.

There are many ways of obtaining local weather forecasts, and every year they improve. Telephone, radio and TV reports are among those available. Some day it may be standard procedure for all racing boats, even small ones, to carry radios. We normally have no radio on the *Flame*; for one thing, there is too much else to do, and for another, the forecasts do not include enough detailed wind information to make it worthwhile for a race of ordinary length. We were once helped, however, by taking a portable radio on a long-distance race. During a slow drift down Long Island Sound we were able to receive hourly reports on the health of a feeble southerly which was blowing in New York City but not on the Sound. Finally we heard that it had strengthened enough so that we thought it might break through to our vicinity. We edged over even farther to the south than the other boats (all of us had been favoring the south all day), and just at the critical moment when we had sailed ourselves so far off the course that we began to look silly, along came friend southerly and picked us up first.

You should get the latest report before leaving the clubhouse for the starting line. Airports give out the most satisfactory forecasts for yachting use because they include a prognostication of the wind for the next two hours. If there is a nearby airport which does not object to being telephoned for a forecast, it will be worth vour dime to take advantage of it.

All such information is to be added to your own store for the day, to be called into use when applicable.

Because a thundersquall may play a deciding role if it arrives during a race, you should know when to expect one. The weather bureau and the U.S. Coast Guard tend to be alarmists about squalls because of the potential danger involved. If there is the remotest chance of a thundersquall it will be mentioned in the forecast. Actually most hot summer afternoons provide *some* chance of a local thundersquall. This chance is greatest if you are located in the southerly sector of a low or near a front. If the day is very hot and a front is coming, then thunderstorms are almost certain to accompany it. Sometimes they take the form of "line squalls." Practically speaking a line squall *is* a front, and behind it the barometer may rise with attendant fair weather and northwest winds. Thundersqualls, especially line squalls, can be very vicious on our inland lakes. On the eastern seaboard they lose some of their punch. They can still be nasty, occasionally very nasty; but usually you can sail through them without trouble. They pose a tough problem: you can see a storm coming, and it looks pretty black and scary. Should you abandon the race and maybe lose the series, only to have it turn out to be a mild squall? Or should you try to sail through it and risk capsizing? Only you can answer this question, each time it arises. But if you decide to sail through it, always head *toward* the squall. The wind will shift so that it blows from the black storm-cloud toward you; hence you will not only get the new wind first but will also have the weather berth if you work your way toward the oncoming squall. Very many squalls are mild and soon blow themselves out, leaving near-calm conditions in which to finish the race. If this happens the fleet will become spread out and the race will be decided during the height of the squall.

Don't be too disturbed by the forecaster's "Chance of scattered local thunderstorms in the late afternoon or evening."

He is playing it safe. Keep an eye always on the western sky on a hot afternoon, just in case; but ordinary summer cumulus or "tower clouds" frequently get very thick and black without being thunderheads. The typical thundercloud has an anvil-shaped outline when viewed from a distance. And if it is so close to you that you can't see the outline, you won't have to ask whether a thundersquall is coming: a wall of really menacing black clouds spouting lightning flashes and thunderclaps leaves no room for doubt.

As you learn to forecast the racing weather, don't expect to call it right every time. No one can do that. If you can be right substantially more than half the time you will do better than the majority of your competitors. The weather, working for you instead of against you, can prove a powerful ally. A knowledge of its caprices will allow you to make many correct decisions, with attendant beneficial results to your racing score.

CHAPTER 11

The Rules

It is alarming to discover how few skippers, even good ones, are well acquainted with the racing rules. The rules are not hard to learn or understand. You can scarcely get along without a thorough knowledge of them. Yet most racing men handicap themselves in this important area by their unwillingness to devote a few hours to the subject. If you are not a rules expert, it would pay you to make the rules a project for next winter—or next week. Once you have mastered them, you will no longer be frightened by necessary close maneuvering. Whenever tricky situations arise you will be in a position to know *instantly* what your rights are; and the word is italicized for good reason: there is never any time to debate the merits of the case on the spot.

If even the racing skippers are shaky on the rules, it goes without saying that most race committee men are shakier still. Whenever you go into a hearing, be fully equipped with an airtight case and be able to quote accurately the applicable rule. You will find that some of the members of the committee, not through malice but through lack of knowledge of the facts and the rules, have formed a pre-conceived decision before they have even heard your case. It is sometimes most difficult to set them right without losing your temper—particularly if you happen to know that they are wrong. But committees are made up of honest men, honestly trying to reach the right decision. They abhor protests to begin with, and anything you can do to help them in a tactful way will be appreciated. The only times I have known committees to become arbitrary and dictatorial are the occasions on which they are protested for something which they, the committee, have done wrong. When you protest the committee you have your work cut out for you: the odds against your winning are high.

I shall make no attempt to analyse the whole rule book. This has been ably done for the North American Yacht Racing Union rules by Robert N. Bavier, Jr., the Union's secretary,* and very thoroughly for the *old* International Yacht Racing Union rules by George E. Hills.** What I should like to do is to call attention to a few special situations which, to the best of my knowledge, have never reached an appeals board and which are not in my opinion at present adequately covered in the rules. All the following problems except No. 5 can arise equally under NAYRU or new IYRU rules. Most of them have come to my notice because they have actually happened to the *Flame*.

1. POOR LUFFING DETERMINATIVE AT CLOSE-REACH STARTS (NAYRU rule 8; IYRU rule 31, 2). A race was supposed to start to windward with a beat to the first mark in a northwester. Just before the start the wind shifted so far to the west that the left hand end of the line became violently favored and it was no longer possible to cross on the starboard tack. Thus it was essentially a reaching start, but close-hauled, on the port tack. We had gone to some pains to put *Flame* in the position shown in Figure 15, so that, by trimming sails to close-hauled, we would be able to pass just to leeward of the flag with no room for anyone else in between. The gun went off, and as we were about to harden up to freeze out the windward boat, *B—m-r-ng,* her skipper, Mr. T-dd, firmly advised us not to head above the first mark. It had not until this moment occurred to me that under the new wind conditions

* THE NEW YACHT RACING RULES, Robert N. Bavier, Jr., W. W. Norton & Co., Inc., New York.

** THE SAILING RULES IN YACHT RACING, George E. Hills, Charles Scribner's Sons, New York (Revised edition, 1940).

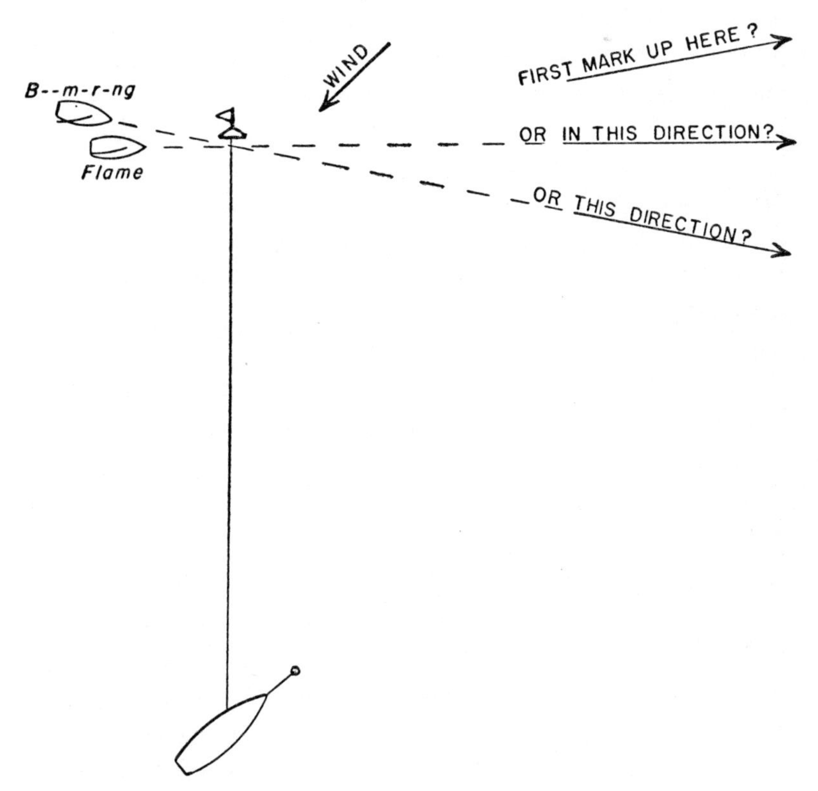

Figure 15. The starting gun has just been fired.

the first leg might indeed not be a true windward leg. In point of fact it was one. We could not lay the first mark on the port tack, even at the start; but we didn't know that because we couldn't see the mark, two miles away against a beach with houses. If it was a beat, we could head up to full and by; if it was not a beat, we could luff only as high as the mark. Where, precisely, was the mark? No one knew. Not wishing to get into trouble we gave way and let the *B—m-r-ng* in. Had we not done so, a very difficult protest would have resulted. One of the big advantages of the "new" rules over the old is that the determinatives have been made more definite. Here, it seems, is a theoretically definite one which in practice may turn out to be not so definite. For that matter, on *any* reaching start how are you going to know when to terminate your "freezing out" luff? It would seem that the position of the first mark of the course would seldom be sufficiently accurately known to a small racing boat to make it a good determinative. I have no better determinative to offer. An improvement perhaps might be a clause stating which way to lean in case of doubt. The rule makers dislike these clauses, because they hate to admit that they have framed a rule in such a way as to afford any doubt.

2. ROOM AT MARKS (NAYRU rule 3; IYRU rule 31, 1(a)). The question here concerns room at a jibing mark on a very windy day. The skipper of a small boat, especially a dinghy, may be unable or unwilling to risk a jibe, electing to round up and go about instead. Suppose now that two boats are overlapped at such a mark, and the outside boat, preparing to jibe, is unaware that the inside one wants to go about. Since the outside boat is in exactly the position which balks the planned maneuver of the inside boat, a serious collision is likely to occur. Even if it doesn't, they sail on past the mark at top speed, half out of control, side by side and dangerously near together, shouting at each other. Who has the right of way? (Fig. 16.) I do not even hazard a guess. The inside boat is supposed to

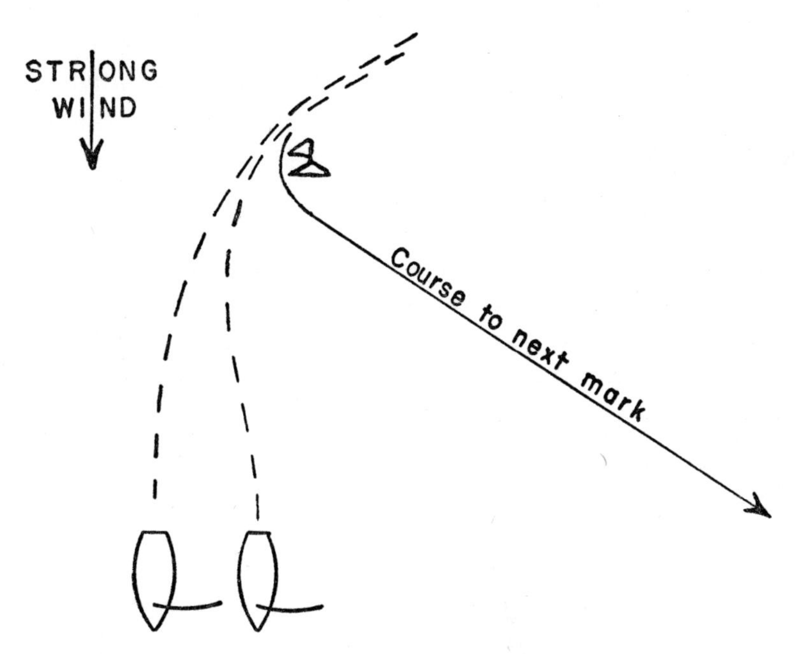

Figure 16. "Dangerously near together, shouting at each other."

be allowed *room to round* the mark, and in her opinion she is not getting it; yet the outside boat has given more than enough room—for a jibe.

3. LOST EQUIPMENT. How often have you heard the statement, "We lost the spinnaker pole overboard," (or, to be more precise, "The stupid fore-deck crew dropped the spinnaker pole overboard"), "and we had to go back for it or we would have been disqualified for finishing without all of our equipment." The "rule" that a boat must finish with all the gear and equipment she started with is one of the unfounded myths of yacht racing. No such rule exists. Of course there is some *specific* equipment which you must carry aboard at all times, usually prescribed by your class rules: anchor, life preservers and the like. But except for these items, must you finish with everything you started with? The Royal Yachting Association* has answered this question with a flat "no." (Part 2 of Case 32, 1955.) You could, for example, lose your entire rig, spars and sails over the side, cut them away, and drift across the finish line without them. You must, however, recover a lost crew member before continuing in the race.**

4. GOVERNMENT MARKS. Suppose the race circular provides that all government marks must be passed on the channel side. Can you hit one, provided you leave it on the proper hand? It is not a mark of the course; yet most skippers feel that it should be treated as if it were. One finds nothing in the rules that prescribes disqualification for hitting anything except a mark of the course or another boat racing. You may hit the shore or an obstruction: why not a government mark? Never-

* The Royal Yachting Association, hereafter referred to as the R.Y.A., is the British national yachting authority. Its Council is the court of highest appeal for cases under the International Yacht Racing Union (IYRU) rules in the English-speaking world. Inasmuch as the IYRU has no council of its own, the R.Y.A. Council takes its place, and its decisions are considered as authoritative as the rules themselves.

** Unless racing under R.Y.A. modification of the IYRU rules, (footnote to rule 19), in which case he had better be a good swimmer.

theless I do not want to be the one who tests this theory before a race committee in an important series.

5. FINISH LINE (NAYRU first definition). Under a recent (1953) change, the NAYRU now requires that the finish line be crossed "from the direction of the last mark. If the committee boat, either from necessity or error, is anchored on the side of a . . . finish mark opposite to that indicated in the instructions, a yacht can . . . finish properly only if she complies with the preceding sentence " I have been objecting to this change from the time of its proposal, for what I consider a good reason. It is the old question of a positive, as against a vague, determinative. Under the old North American and the current IYRU rule, there is no shadow of a doubt how to cross a "backward" finish line. If the mark and the committee boat are in the wrong respective positions, you simply do an "end run" around the mark and cross the line from the other side in order to leave it on the proper hand (Fig. 17). After long years and many lessons, yachtsmen had finally learned to do this, so that it was common practice whenever the line was wrong. But note that the new determinative, supposed to be more "natural," is *indefinite* whenever the finish line happens, through error, to become lined up with the last leg of the course. In this case there is literally no way to decide how to cross it.

Before the 1953 changes were effected, proposed changes were widely circulated and comment was invited by the Racing Rules committee of the NAYRU. I entered into a spirited correspondence with the (then) Chairman of that committee. The file of our letters runs to more than 30 single-spaced typed pages. Most of my suggestions took the form of objections to the changes, because I do not believe that any code of rules, however faulty, should be in a continual state of flux. No sooner do the racing people learn the rules than they are changed again. Apparently others felt the same, because all of the objections were most courteously considered and some of the

Windward - leeward

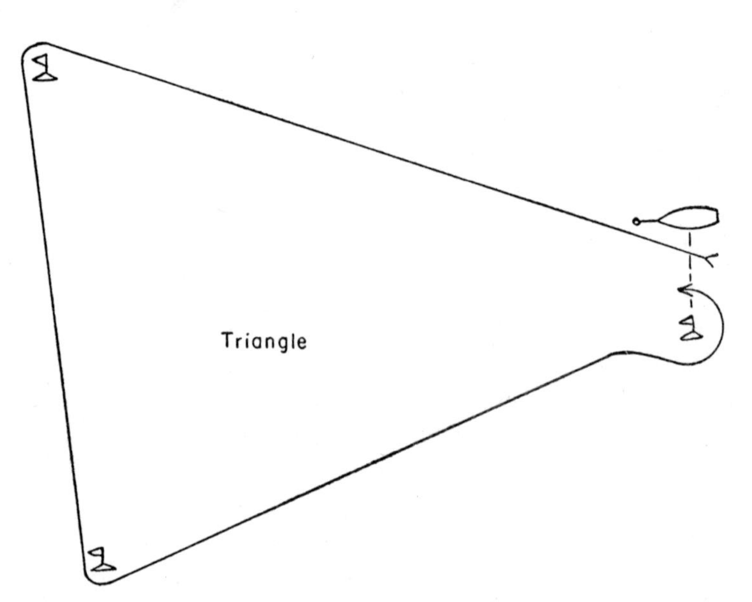

Figure 17. How to cross a "backward" finish line under International rules. This is NOT the way to do it under American rules.

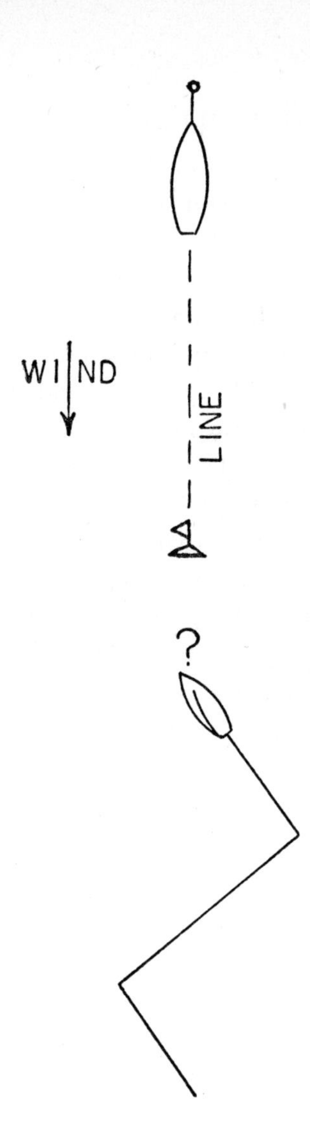

DIRECTION OF
LAST MARK

Figure 18. Which way would you cross this finish line under North American rules?

proposed changes were never made. But on the question of the finish line they were adamant, despite our predictions of exactly what would happen, which have turned out to be correct.

In a race of the 1956 season a skipper, finishing first, approached a finish line which was so precisely aimed toward the last mark that it was a toss-up which way to cross it (Fig. 18). With nothing else to guide him, he decided that the best bet would be to leave the finish marker on the same hand as the other marks of the course. He crossed the line in the direction which did so, and was disqualified. He should have appealed the decision: it would seem that the only fair solution of this dilemma would have been to allow *either* direction to constitute a legal finish. The NAYRU has recently ruled (on another question): "When a reasonable doubt exists as to an interpretation of an instruction, we hold that it must be resolved in favor of a contestant. . . ." * The case under discussion does not, to be sure, hinge on "an interpretation of an instruction;" but certainly "a reasonable doubt exists."

In a similar situation I recently approached a finish line from a last mark which we had left five miles behind us, across a tideway, in a haze which limited the visibility to a couple of miles at most. I should be much obliged if the North American Yacht Racing Union would tell me how in the ever-loving blue-eyed world I am supposed to know the direction of the last mark under these conditions. The marker end of the line was the far end, hidden from us by the committee boat which was lined up between the flag and our direction of approach. The wind was so light that we were able to hail the committee and ask how to finish. The directions they gave us (in a tone of voice which implied that we were pretty stupid not to know), were to cross in the opposite way to that which I was about to select in the absence of instructions. The day I am disqualified

* NAYRU Appeal No. 66, 1956.

for crossing such a finish line the wrong way will see an appeal lodged in the next mail and carried through to the top authority. It will probably be denied by the NAYRU, but not until I have had a chance to make some noise. I refuse to be convinced that when a rules body imposes an impossible determinative it has any right to disqualify anybody for making a "wrong" decision under that determinative.

CHAPTER 12

NAYRU and IYRU

Many (but not all) American regattas are run under the racing rules of the North American Yacht Racing Union. Since 1948 these have differed from those of the International Yacht Racing Union. The International rules are in use in all countries except the U.S., and are the rules under which the races of the Olympic Games and indeed any international regatta must be sailed. For this reason the Star Class has always used the International rules for all its major regattas. (In 1956 a starting field of 59 boats in the World's Championship contained only 6 from the United States.) Any other truly international class must obviously do the same. The unfortunate result of this is that many U.S. yachtsmen are forced to be familiar with two codes of rules: they sometimes race under one code, sometimes the other. Many Star fleets in the U.S. have never used anything but the International rules locally, hoping thus to avoid the NAYRU entirely; but the fact remains that anyone who travels from such a fleet to other parts of the U.S. to race must sooner or later encounter the North American rules.

Fortunately a big step toward the re-unification of the rules was taken not long ago when the IYRU adopted some of the best principles of the NAYRU, notably the anti-barging rule. At a conference in London in 1956, further progress was indicated. The report of the American delegate in *Yachting* magazine for December, 1956, was restrained, but expressed the cautious hope that world-wide uniformity might be achieved by 1959 or 1960.

Meanwhile, many minor differences and some major ones still exist. It is felt that a comparison of these differences would be of value to all those yachtsmen who are confronted with the current dual situation. In the listing which follows I have not considered *all* the differences. It seems unnecessarily cumbersome to comment on some of the procedural differences, such as the routines prescribed for lodging protests, because these rules can be consulted at leisure when the situations arise. I have tried to list all the major differences, those which affect the actual sailing of the race; but even here something may have been overlooked. Also please note that all comparisons and comments are strictly unofficial: I am not a member of any of the rule-making bodies or appeals boards. If I were I should doubtless not be so free with my opinions. But fools rush in, of course, so here we go.

There are many differences in the definitions. To list them all would only confuse the issue, because sometimes two different rules, coupled with the corresponding definitions, result in the same meaning or intent. Thus I have tried to concentrate on only those definitions which in themselves constitute rules.

RIGHT OF WAY RULES

North American	*International*
Starboard tack free has right of way over port tack close-hauled. (1)	Port tack close-hauled has right of way over starboard tack free. (30-4(a))

This is the biggest single remaining difference between the two codes of rules, and is one of the few situations in which they are directly opposed to one another. There are arguments on both sides, of course; but it is not my intention here to become embroiled in the merits of either set of rules. Such a discussion would take us too far afield and would gain us little.

Throughout this listing the left hand column will continue

to refer to the North American rule, the right hand column to the nearest corresponding International rule.

Before the start, a leeward yacht may luff *whenever* in "mast line position." (7)	Before the start, the conditions on *getting into* position to luff are the same as after the start. (29-1(a))

"Mast line position," (my own abbreviation), means that the helmsman of the windward yacht is abaft the mainmast of the leeward yacht. If the leeward yacht is farther aft than that, she can *never* start a luff. But out on the course, after the start, she can be in mast line position and yet *not* be entitled to start a luff. It depends on how she got there (see Rule 10). The IYRU situation is the same: mast line is not mentioned, but the other determinative (leeward boat's bow forward of weather boat's mast) is roughly equivalent. Again, an "overtaking" boat (see IYRU rule 30-2(a)) is not entitled to luff *even if* in this position. And herein lies the difference: in the IYRU rules the luffing privilege is no different before the start; in the NAYRU rules the luffing privilege is somewhat broader before the start. Note, however, that under both codes you may luff only slowly before the start.

Bearing away to prevent an overtaking boat from passing to leeward is forbidden. (11 and def. of normal course)	The same, forbidden with one exception. (30-3(a) and 27-8)

The exception under IYRU is that if you can justify a more leeward course for reasons "other than the desire to hinder," you may bear away; but the burden of proof of such justification is on you, the weather boat. Under American rules you must make up your mind about any "other reasons" for bearing away *before* the passing situation develops. While the leeward boat is close by (see Rule 11 for how close), you are frozen on the course you were pursuing before the beginning of the overtaking incident. One suspects that it would be difficult, even under IYRU rules, to convince a protest committee that you suddenly happened to think of some other reason for bearing off just as another boat was trying to pass to leeward.

Tacking too close. You must be on your new course, after tacking and filling away, in time so that, *beginning then,* the other boat can get out of your way without colliding. (6 and def. of tacking)	Proper way must be established. (30-5(a)i and 27-6)

"Proper way" is one of the big objections to the IYRU rules. Nobody knows quite what proper way is. But even under the most lenient construction it would appear that you cannot tack quite so close under International rules as you can under North American.

Hailing about for an obstruction: a right-of-way yacht is like a mark of the course. (4)	A right-of-way yacht is like any other obstruction *not* a mark of the course. (32-1)

American rules: on the port tack, coverging with a starboard tack boat, you cannot hail another windward port tack boat about to give you room to tack *if* the other port tack boat can fetch the starboard tack boat; International rules: you can. See figure 19.

Normal course before the start: after gunfire you must steer a course "to finish as quickly as possible." (Def.)	After gunfire you must steer a course "consistent with the intention of crossing the line." (29-1(b))

The International rule is much the more liberal. It allows you to maintain a course after gunfire on which you cannot fetch *any* part of the line (*e.g.* a tack is required to get across). Three times in recent years the R.Y.A. Council has reaffirmed a boat's right to hold a course other than that which would carry her most quickly across the starting line. The reasons

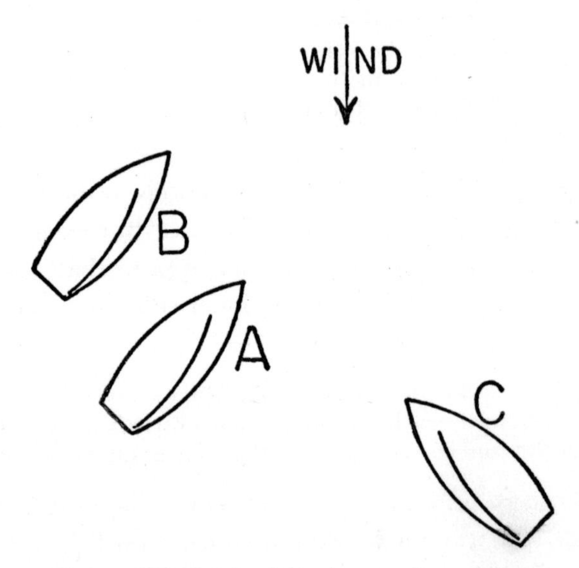

Figure 19. North American rules: *A* may not hail *B* about, because *B* can clear *C*. International rules: *A* may hail *B* about.

Don Wolter

A radially cut jib.

A mainsail with two windows.

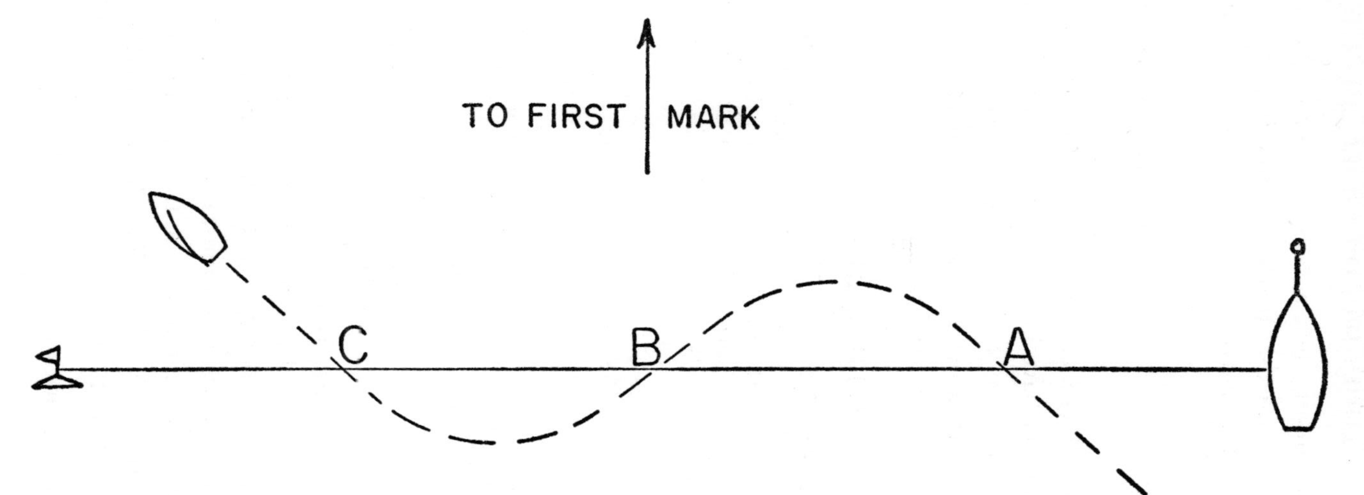

Figure 20. A boat starting prematurely loses her rights at gun fire (at *A* or shortly thereafter.) Under International rules she regains them at *B;* under North American, at *C*.

for wishing to maintain such a course are of course tactical: to wit, upsetting the starting plans of competitors.*

A yacht which has started prematurely is deprived of all rights until she

starts again (9)

returns across the line, preparatory to starting again. (22-5)

This is a major difference. Under International rules, if you are over too soon you have but to dip back across the line, or return across its extension, to regain your rights. Under American rules you are still a dead duck until you not only return but also re-cross in the *right* direction (Fig. 20).

OTHER RULES

Rounding the course: "A yacht . . . shall pass or round each mark on the required side in proper sequence. If, after starting, she initially passes a mark on the wrong side, she must return and repass on the same side of it before passing on the required side of it." (13)

"A yacht shall go fairly round the course, rounding or passing the series of marks on the proper hand and in the correct order, as specified in the sailing instructions; and, in order to round or pass each mark, the yacht's track from the preceding to the following mark shall enclose it in such a manner that a string representing her wake from the time she starts until she finishes the course would, when drawn taut, lie on the required side of each mark." (28-1)

At first glance these two rules look the same. Although the reference to the string has been omitted from the North American rule, it is nevertheless implied. Under both codes, if you round a mark the wrong way you must first "unwind" and then "re-wind" the right way. (Note that the present wording of the rule vitiates the principle under which NAYRU Appeal No. 13 was decided in 1941.)

* Case 37, 1955; Cases 13 and 20, 1956.

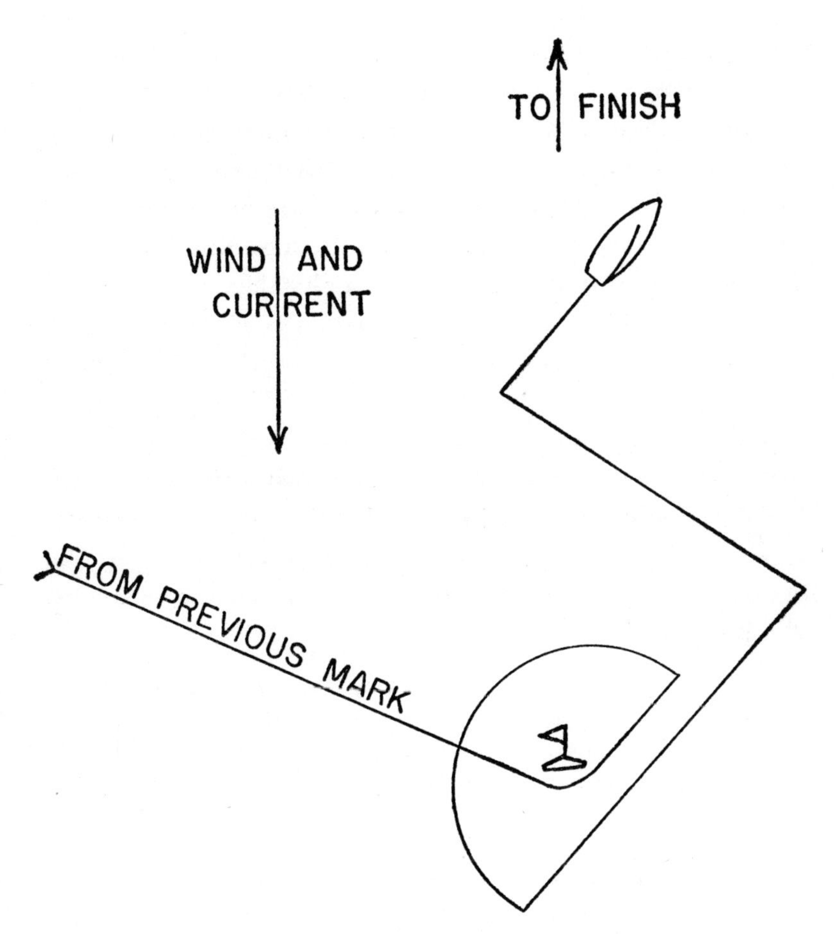

Figure 21. All marks to be left to port. Is this course legal?

In fact, however, all mention of the string was omitted from the NAYRU rule for a very good reason. Suppose a yacht rounds a mark of the course the right way, tacks, drifts backwards in a current or for any other reason past the mark on the other side, and when she gets finally reorganized, passes the mark a second time on the required side. Figure 21 illustrates the situation. Under NAYRU rules there is nothing wrong with this. But under IYRU rules, the string, when drawn taut, would lie on the required side of the mark *but also* on the other side. The rule does not state that the taut string must lie *only* on the required side; but if it means only, then the course of Figure 21 would be illegal. This situation rarely develops. But a similar one at the starting line happens all the time: a yacht makes a good start at the marker end but thinks (erroneously) that she is over to soon; so she makes a quick circuit of the flag and starts again. Because all this happened after gunfire, the first start counts, and she has rounded the flag once too often. It is doubtful whether an IYRU committee would consider this cause for disqualification; but it was to avoid the possibility that the NAYRU omitted the string.

Definition of a mark includes the underwater parts thereof (but not the mark's ground tackle). (Def.)	Only the "essential above-water parts" of the mark constitute the mark. (27-16(b)i)

This change in the NAYRU rules dates from 1953. It was made partly to discourage the sea-lawyers from reaching underwater and holding the boat away from a mark when contact impended. Such an operation would now be illegal anyway under both codes, because way may not "be checked by abnormal means." (NAYRU 30, IYRU 24.)

A yacht is not across the starting (or finish) line until her mast crosses. (Def.)	A yacht crosses the starting (or finish) line as soon as any part of the yacht crosses. (22-2)

I have no comment on this difference except in connection with the next one.

"After finishing, a yacht shall keep clear of the finish line and the last leg of the course." (12)	After finishing, a yacht must keep clear of other yachts racing. (34-2)

Under the NAYRU definition, a yacht *has finished* when her mainmast has crossed the finish line; yet for a measurable period of time after that, until her transom crosses, she is *not* clear of the line, and is consequently violating Rule 12! It is hardly necessary to point out that the rule framers did not intend to disqualify every boat in every race. We have apparently caught them out in this wording.

A difficulty arises under Rule 12 which is less frivolous than the one just suggested. A boat which manages to get her mainmast, or even the whole boat, across the line in very light airs has finished. She then drifts back onto the last leg of the course, and subsequently a wind comes up and she gets under way. She is now under full control, but is still on the last leg of the course and hence violating Rule 12 due to circumstances entirely beyond her control. The IYRU version would appear preferable here. It seems probable that the North American rule is another of those "race committee rules" designed not so much to protect other boats racing as to get the finished boats out of the line of sight of the race committee.

The next difference concerns the direction of crossing the finish line. For discussion see No. 5 of the previous chapter.

Disqualification shall be waived "if a becalmed yacht touches a mark through no fault of her own." (14)	No such waiver (28)

I am afraid I belong to the old school which believes that it is *always* your own fault if you hit a mark all by yourself in the absence of other boats. The trouble with the waiver is that it is an invitation to stretch a point and claim that you are becalmed when you lose steerageway in very light air through trying unsuccessfully to pinch around the mark. But this is a matter of opinion, and I promised not to voice preferences but simply to point out differences in the two codes of rules.

The course may be changed any time up to 3 minutes before the start. (40-b)	The course may be changed any time up to 15 minutes before the start. (6-2)

This has been discussed in Chapter 3.

"Failure to notify a yacht of her premature start shall not relieve her of the necessity of making a proper start." (45)	No such sentence. (22-2)

The R.Y.A. has ruled that, in the absence of a clause obligating a yacht to detect her own premature start, no such obligation exists under IYRU rules. "If the sailing committee fails to give a suitable sound signal to call the attention of competing yachts to the fact that recall numbers are being displayed, there is no onus upon a yacht to return." * This, mind you, despite the fact that your number is up there on the board, large as life, for you to read if you choose to look at it. Note, however, that if the sound signal is in fact given and the recalled yacht fails to hear it, she is disqualified.

No rule.	A right of way yacht may be disqualified for failure to avoid a collision. (29-4)

The obligation of a right-of-way yacht to do its utmost to avoid a serious collision has been relegated to Proprieties (a) of the NAYRU code, and disqualification is not the penalty for violating a propriety. Rule 29-4 is not often invoked, but a case in point is R.Y.A. Case 10 for 1953, dealing with a port and starboard collision of two dinghies. No danger to life was in-

* R.Y.A. Case 22, 1953.

volved, but serious damage to both boats resulted from the collision. Neither had seen the other approaching. The port tack boat withdrew at once, and the race committee threw out the starboard tack boat. Her appeal was disallowed by the Council, which said in part: "It is not a 'custom of the sea' for a vessel holding right of way to neglect to keep a proper lookout at all times. *Allouette's* failure to observe this elementary principle of seamanship inevitably results in her disqualification." Again, in Case 1, 1955, a yacht was disqualified, though holding right of way, for failure to avoid a collision which only *might have resulted* in serious damage but in fact did not.

There is an Appendix to the IYRU rules, framed by the R.Y.A., which contains an error, in recommendation No. 2: "The starting line should be as nearly as possible at right angles to the first leg of the course." That this is wrong for every windward start where the first leg is not a dead beat is well known to all skippers but remains a mystery to most race committee personnel. If the first leg is to weather; and if the first mark is ever so slightly to one side of dead to windward, so that the leg consists of more work on one tack than on the other; then the starting line should be laid not across the *course* but across the *wind*. This has all been explained many times, with diagrams, in technicolor, including hot and cold folding reasons—the full treatment. Rather than repeat it here I refer you to pages 104-5 of SUCCESSFUL YACHT RACING.

CHAPTER 13

Sails

About five years ago there burst upon the yacht racing world a bomb called Synthetic Sails. Its blast is still being felt. Although more becomes known about the synthetics every year, very much remains to be learned. After a century of practice in making yacht sails of cotton duck, the sailmakers had at last become expert in the art. Imagine their consternation when they discovered that most of their hard-won secrets had to be thrown into the ashcan and that they must start all over again from scratch to learn how to make sails from the new materials. Some refused to do so, and rapidly dropped out of the yacht racing trade. The synthetics have proved a boon to younger sailmakers new at the game: without prejudices to overcome they are open-minded regarding new techniques and are able to develop winning sails sometimes more rapidly than old-timers who have to begin by unlearning many of their cherished methods.

In 1946 there was a sudden return to yachting after World War II and a resulting shortage in the supply of Egyptian cotton. Sailmakers tried to substitute nylon, but that was a failure. Nylon has too much stretch for working sails. It is still used successfully for spinnakers only. The sailmakers returned with some relief to their old favorite cotton duck for mainsails and jibs and settled down to make good sails with it, hoping that no further disturbances would be caused by experimental materials. But this was not to be. About 1951 there was developed by the E.I. duPont de Nemours Co. a material called orlon, and the following year dacron. By 1953 both were being used extensively for sailcloth. When I refer to "the synthetics" hereafter I shall mean these two materials. There may be others with which I am not familiar. In the future there will almost certainly be many others, some of which will make better sails than orlon or dacron.

The synthetics showed their superiority first in the smallest classes and worked up from there. It has now been years since anyone has used a cotton sail in a racing dinghy in hot competition. The very large classes have been slow to make the change. For one thing, one does not lightly discard the thousands of dollars worth of cotton sails which comprise the sail inventory of an ocean racer. For another, the big boats don't seem to be severely handicapped by continuing to use cotton sails against those few who have adopted synthetics. It is worth noting, however, that in 1956 Hard Sails, Inc., of Islip, Long Island, built a dacron mainsail for Mahlon Dickerson's 12-Metre *Gleam*. This sail, said to be the largest ever constructed of synthetic material up to that time, has been a success.

In the Star Class the superiority of the new materials was clearly demonstrated in 1953. In that season some but not all Stars were using them. Some of the most beautiful sails in the 1953 North American Championship of the class were made of Egyptian cotton. Against these superb sails, which had been tried and proved fast in many previous events, Robert Lippincott entered the series with a mainsail full of wrinkles, hard spots and bumps. It was difficult to believe that it would move the boat. He used this wretched-looking sail in every race, and with it *he won the championship*. The sail was synthetic; no further argument was needed in favor of the new material. That sail has long since been outbuilt. Since then, the sailmakers have learned better how to cut the stuff, and synthetic sails look smoother and get faster every year as the techniques improve.

The methods used to cut synthetic material into racing sails are quite different from those used on duck. The material is much less elastic than duck. A sailmaker once told me that the synthetics have from one-tenth to one-twentieth of the stretch of duck. Assuming that a duck sail might stretch with use as much as 5% in any one lineal dimension (a rather liberal figure), this means that the same sail made of synthetic material would not stretch more than one-half of one percent, an almost unmeasurable amount. A cotton sail "works into shape" as it is used, the material giving and taking here and there to compensate for small errors in cutting. This is part of the breaking in process, and is one reason why a cotton sail improves with use. But practically no give and take occurs with the synthetics. It is easy to see why the task of cutting such a sail is correspondingly more delicate and difficult. If it is wrong to begin with it will stay wrong, and no amount of sailing will right it.

A synthetic requires no breaking in. Sailing it for 20 hours or 120 hours won't affect its shape at all. So take it out and race it the day you get it, in strong wind or light, rain or shine. It's impervious to water too: a damp day will not hurt it any more than a dry one.

Why are the synthetics superior to cotton duck? The record indicates that even a poorly cut synthetic is as good as the best cotton sail, so it is not a question of cut. The only thing left to consider is the material itself, and this brings us to examine the surface. The surface of the synthetic materials is much smoother than that of duck. It appears to be *decreased surface friction* that accounts for the superiority of the synthetic cloths.

It was a long time before I could bring myself to believe that it was all a question of surface friction, but I was finally driven to it by the obvious fact that it could be nothing else. And now the evidence to support this contention continues to pile up.

There is a story, supposed to be authentic, about a certain

experimental seaplane.* This plane made a reasonably satisfactory first trial flight but its engines seemed sluggish. A mechanical modification was indicated and some essential parts were ordered from the factory. While the plane waited for the new engine parts it sat in the hangar, untouched for six weeks. At last the redesigned parts arrived and were installed and the plane was taken out for a second trial. This time it would not get off the water. Despite the pilot's every effort the plane refused to fly, which astonished everybody because the new engines were supposed to be more powerful than the originals. The seaplane was finally taxied back to the ramp, and as it rested there someone made a brilliant observation. I hope he was promoted. He noticed that the tops of the wings were covered with the dust of six idle weeks in the hangar. Even the wind of motion had been insufficient to blow it off. When the wing surfaces had been cleaned, the plane flew.

The lesson for us is a striking one. If dust can cause so much turbulence that it destroys a wing's lift, think of the importance of a smooth sail. The principle has been reaffirmed many times in the aircraft industry. Guy Murchie reports that just by smoothing out the rivet-heads on the skin of an airplane the designers were able to give that plane so much more efficiency in the form of increased lift that four paying passengers could be added to an Atlantic crossing. "Thus the engineering curse is solved by smoothness, by a pure slipperiness that lets the airplane slide ahead faster through the sticky air, lets each pound of gasoline drive it farther, leaves more room for payload, stretches the range two or three fold." **

A possible explanation now suggests itself as to why the synthetics, so uniformly successful on the smallest boats, have not proved essential in the larger cruising and ocean racing classes.

* C. T. Ludington, "Just One Little Thing," *Motor Boating*, December, 1955; an article on the aerodynamics of sails worthy of your study.

** Guy Murchie, SONG OF THE SKY, p. 326 (Houghton Mifflin, Boston, 1954).

Apparently in a large sail the smoothness factor is not so important. Perhaps the eddies, being larger to begin with, are not so much affected and hence less additional turbulence is built up by roughness of surface. There may, of course, be other reasons about which we know nothing. Also let us be ever on guard against too readily adapting *any* aircraft theory, with its velocities up in the hundreds of miles an hour, to our pedestrian speeds which rarely exceed ten knots.

A realization of the importance of surface smoothness sheds new light on the old question of why a cotton sail improves with age. You will surely recall one of your own cotton sails which always used to be your "old faithful," seeming to do better every time you used it. Many examples of such time-tested sails could be cited. The explanation lies partly in the breaking-in process, to be sure; the sail is not "right" until it is thoroughly broken in. But more than that, the fuzz or *nap* of a cloth sail, those thousands of little microscopic fiber ends that stick out all over it when it is new, gradually wear off, until an old sail has practically no nap.

Observe that synthetic materials have no nap to start with. Besides, the weave is finer because the cloth can be lighter thanks to the increased strength of the material. It is the combined effect of these two factors which renders the sail smoother and, until a better explanation turns up, must be credited for the superiority of the synthetic materials.*

A final argument in support of the theory that extreme smoothness is all-important has only recently presented itself, and it is an unwelcome thought indeed in view of the high cost of sails. Orlon and dacron acquire their final finish through a process called *calendering*. As I understand it (and I probably don't), the cloth is calendered by being forced through the rollers backwards, that is, with the rollers spinning in the di-

* See also an article entitled *Light on the Sailcloth Problem* by Thomas Lingard and F. Ward Paine, *Yachting*, April 1957.

rection opposite to the motion of the bolt of material, which of course creates a high temperature and imparts the glaze that looks like a waxed surface. This surface is absolutely smooth when new; but like any other stiff surface it cracks with age, developing thousands of little visible creases within the first season. These cracks noticeably roughen the surface; and unfortunately it begins to look as if they also slow the sail, as would be expected. When the synthetics first appeared on the scene they cost more than duck sails. They still do; but the argument put forward by the sailmakers was that they ought to outlast cotton because of increased stability and longer wearing qualities, and hence be more economical in the long run. If this dream is to be shattered by the cracking problem, let us hope that a new process may soon be developed to beat the cracks. Progress is so rapid in the synthetic field that such a process may be an accomplished fact by the time these lines appear in print.

The lack of elasticity of the new materials has accentuated what was always a serious problem in the cutting of both mainsails and jibs, none other than our old friend, or enemy, the hard leech. When a cotton working jib is sheeted down hard a heavy strain is transmitted to the leech, which stretches accordingly. In light airs the strain goes off and the sail takes up the slack, returning most accommodatingly to its original shape. A synthetic sail cannot stretch enough on the leech, where stretch is most needed, to keep the batten section soft. Thus nearly all synthetic jibs develop a hard leech in a breeze, the sail taking on a barrel-shaped curve when it is least wanted. Cutting the jib with seams widely eased at the after end may make it perform satisfactorily in heavy weather to windward; but as soon as the breeze lets up or the sheet is eased for reaching the leech falls off very badly. The material fails to take up the slack as in a cotton sail and the whole batten section "breaks," ruining the flow of air off the trailing edge. An attempt to overcome this difficulty has been the "spider-web" or multi-mitred jib (See page 116). It is a big improvement, although more difficult (and hence more expensive) to make; but those who have tried it say that even these radially cut cloths are not the complete answer.

The problem in mainsails is almost equally drastic. The sailmakers cut the first synthetic sails to the same patterns they had been using for duck, having no way of knowing whether anything different was called for. They were in for a big surprise: the boom cocked too high aft, by one to two feet! No one had realized how much the leech of a cotton sail stretches under the tension of the mainsheet. Those first synthetics had to be junked and bigger ones built. The hard leech problem remained acute for the same reason as in jibs: slacking the leech enough to prevent it from turning to weather when sheeted flat made the whole batten section flop off hopelessly on a reach. There is, however, a remedy for mainsails which is not available for jibs: cut the sail so that it sets properly when sheeted down hard; then to keep the leech from collapsing offwind, lash the boom down with a vang or boom-jack the moment it is eased. A very heavy tension is necessary on the boom-jack. After all, it is not child's play to trim the mainsheet when on the wind in a blow; and you are trying to duplicate that tension offwind with a rig which has an exceedingly disadvantageous leverage at the inboard end of the boom. On Stars we keep breaking booms at the gooseneck: a completely satisfactory boom-jack has yet to be devised for this class.

Some synthetic mainsails are designed to set pretty well offwind without being heavily vanged down. The result of course is a hard leech when sailing to windward. The surprising fact is that such sails often prove very fast, hard leech notwithstanding. It makes one wonder whether an easy leech, traditionally supposed to be indispensable to a good mainsail, is really so essential after all.

Why does an airplane pilot coming in for a landing let down the flaps? In order to obtain added lift. To be sure, he also gets added drag, and the airspeed is reduced; but the lift is so materially increased that the plane can land at a considerably lower speed without stalling out. Now an aircraft's lift is analogous (I do not say identical) to a sailboat's drive. Drag is undesirable for both; but drag increases proportionally not to the velocity but to the square of the velocity; so drag is far less detrimental at the slow speed at which a boat plods through the air than it is to an airplane. A hard batten section is the equivalent of "flaps down." The "flaps down" batten section seems best in the lightest airs. There may be other reasons for this, and I do not necessarily advocate a batten section that turns to windward; but I believe the idea of the flaps down deserves consideration.*

The trim of the sails has a great deal to do with the balance of the boat. By balance I mean the amount of helm when sailing to windward. Is the tiller amidships, or does she have a tendency to turn into the wind (weather helm), or away from the wind (lee helm)? First it should be remarked that a slight weather helm is definitely to be sought after. The reason for this is that by having to turn the rudder to leeward you are providing exactly the effects of flaps down relative to the hydrofoil of the keel-rudder system. Thus the water pushing past the leeward-turned rudder "lifts" the boat gradually to windward, certainly a most desirable result.

Whether the boat has a weather helm, and how much, depends first on the design. The center of effort (C.E.) of the sail plan is approximately vertically above the effective center of lateral resistance (C.L.R.) of the hull. In a well designed boat the C.E. is slightly aft of the C.L.R. to provide the slight

* D. C. Hazen and R. F. Lehnert have published interesting photographs of the effect of the flaps on airflow patterns made visible by smoke trails; *Scientific American,* April, 1956.

desired turning moment to windward. In a centerboard boat, if the C.L.R. seems to be not quite right, it can be adjusted, often most successfully, by fine adjustments fore and aft of the (pivoted) centerboard.

With a keel boat, there is nothing much you can do about the C.L.R. short of re-designing the hull. Hence it is well to know how you can change the C.E. for better balance. It may be possible and legal in your class to move the entire rig bodily fore and aft in the boat. This means moving the mast at the step as well as at the deck, and it must assuredly move the C.E. Suppose you have too much weather helm under a certain condition of wind and water, and you wish to correct it. Moving the rig forward might do it. Some yachtsmen erroneously conclude that they can accomplish the same thing by *raking the mast less aft*. So they try it, only to discover to their dismay that with the mast more plumb in the boat she has a worse weather helm than before! How can this come about?

When the mast is straightened up, or raked forward, the boom goes with it. That is, the sail lifts the boom higher off the deck aft. This means that in trimming the sheet you now pull *down* much harder than before in order to get the sail *in* by an equal amount. We have just seen that this is the treatment that produces a hard leech in a synthetic mainsail. Now it turns out that a hard leech, catching air at the aft end of the sail, is one of the prime causes of strong weather helm. Hence although you tried to move the C.E. forward another more powerful factor moved it aft again. This is an excellent example of what can happen when you make changes by rule of thumb without thinking through all the consequences. Every time you make a change in your sails or rig there will be innumerable minor consequences, many of them unforeseeable. This is why in recent years I have become very crotchety about giving off-the-cuff answers to sudden questions. I am afraid people think "The old s.o.b. is trying to guard secrets." On the contrary, he only wishes not to hand out misinformation. I am a scientist by trade and inclination, and hence have become pretty thoroughly indoctrinated with the folly of ill-considered answers. If I am asked, "what is that line for?" or "Why do you have your spreaders rigged that way?" I am likely to give some non-committal answer or no answer. It might take half an hour to answer properly. Nearly every question about sailing is, in the end, a half-hour question. If your questioner is not willing to sit down and listen, don't attempt to answer him in three words: you'll be sorry later when he comes back with a tale of woe. Above all, beware the questioner who is not really interested in your opinion but only wants you to agree with what he already believes. Pass this fellow off politely but glibly as soon as you discover what he is up to. Talking to him is a waste of time.

I have mentioned that a hard leeched mainsail gives the boat a weather helm. Likewise too full a jib may cause a lee helm. These observations suggest another approach to the balance question: the balance is affected by the *location* of the draft in each sail. A sail acts as if most of its power were concentrated where most of its draft is. Thus a helm may be corrected by recutting sails, or by changing them for others.

In sailing to windward, when a puff hits and the boat heels she tends to turn into the wind. There are three reasons for this, none of which are generally recognized. We mention them not because there is anything one can do about it, but because an understanding of why things happen can, by increasing our knowledge of the mechanics of sailing, sometimes help us in remote and unexpected ways.

(1) When the boat heels, the C.E. moves to *leeward*. Thus the forward thrust imparted to the boat through the mast and rigging, acting at a greater distance to leeward of the hull than

before, has a longer lever arm through which to turn the boat to windward.*

(2) The effect of this turning moment is immediate; the corresponding increase in speed caused by the puff lags behind. Therefore until the boat gets up to the new speed the rudder is proportionately less effective than it was and hence has to be turned more.

(3) Most modern small boats have relatively flat, shallow hulls, convex on both sides in plan. When the boat heels the lee waterline remains convex, but the windward waterline becomes much straighter as part of the hull lifts clear of the water. Thus the hull is no longer symmetrical, but lop-sided in a direction which makes it try to turn to windward.

Effect No. 3 can be used to good advantage in sailing a centerboard boat downwind. On a dead run the boat can be balanced perfectly, so that the helm goes dead, by simply heeling her toward the side on which you are carrying the least sail. On a run, any helm is undesirable, acting only as a brake; this is why you see whole fleets of dinghies running with their main booms cocked up in the air, heeling to windward.**

Not only the location of the draft but *how much* draft a sail should have is an important question in cutting, altering, or ordering a sail. In this connection I present a theory propounded by Owen C. Torrey, Jr., who has been associated with a yacht sailmaking firm as their racing sail designer. It is well known that a full, relatively drafty sail is preferable for light airs; and that as the wind increases, a flatter sail is superior.

* This simple fact of physics never occurred to me until I read it in L. Francis Herreshoff's THE COMMON SENSE OF YACHT DESIGN, p. 146, Vol. I (Rudder Publishing Co., 1948). This book, containing much "common sense," has not received the attention it perhaps deserves. If you enjoy a pungent conversational style, albeit a bit old-fashioned, and a treatment which never begs an issue and frequently leaves you saying to yourself "Now I don't agree with that at all," by all means read it.

** This technique was first published by Arthur Knapp in his book RACE YOUR BOAT RIGHT, (D. Van Nostrand Co., Inc., 1952).

This can be explained by considering the angle of attack. In light or drifting conditions a boat is not at its best. It cannot point as high as it should, and it moves very slowly. These two factors bring the apparent wind aft almost to the direction of the real wind. A full sail, with draft well forward, is thus suited to the wide angle of attack at which the apparent wind meets the leading edge. As the wind increases, the boat not only goes faster but "gets into the groove" and points higher. Thus the apparent wind moves far forward of the real wind, meeting the boat almost head-on and leaving a very narrow angle of attack. The full sail goes half aback under these conditions, and we change to a flatter one. So far so good, and nothing startling has been said. But now suppose the wind picks up even more, until it is blowing harder than the optimum wind for the particular boat in question: in short, there is too much wind. The boat now slows down a little, because the sea has become too rough and because the wind resistance (which has been going up with the square of the velocity) begins to be an effective factor. What is more important, the wind's velocity is higher *relative to* the boat's. These two factors draw the apparent wind aft, which suggests that a full mainsail may now once again be more effective than a flat one. Under certain conditions of high wind and heavy seas this theory has been born out in practice. In waters like the Gulf Stream north of Cuba, where the boat needs lots of drive from the sails, it has been the experience of some small boat skippers that the flattest sails are not the best when it is blowing great guns.

The new sails have one advantage not yet fully exploited by most classes. Because the synthetic material is so stable, it is relatively easy to install a window of 8- or 12-oz. plexiglass at any convenient place in the sail. A window in a racing sail may sound like a joke, and in fact it is inevitably the butt of many wisecracks. ("When do you take that down and put up the screens?" or, from a leeward boat, "How about opening the window and letting in a little air?") But once you have used a window you will never again be without one. Modern small racing boats have either very low-cut genoas, like Snipes and L-16's; or very low-cut mainsails, like Stars; or both, like 110's. In every case there is a blind spot in exactly the most dangerous possible direction: off the lee bow. This is the quarter from which a boat on the opposite tack converges on a collision course. The problem of having to become a double-jointed contortionist every few seconds to check on the situation to leeward is solved by a window either in the genoa or in the main. The picture on page 117 shows a mainsail with two windows.

Never forget that your sails are your power plant. You should be satisfied with nothing but the best. And in the end it is *you* who will decide whether they are the best or not, and it may be you who puts the finishing touches into them to obtain that last ounce of perfection. As much with the sails as with the other three elements of the team (hull, crew and skipper) you are the doctor. The sailmaker has done all he can do when he delivers to you his top product; the rest is up to you. The local racing expert may be able to help you a little if your sails are not right; but he is one of the people you are trying to beat. You must learn more about sails than he knows. You must become your own expert.

CHAPTER 14

The Purpose of It All

It is probably heresy to wind up a racing discussion on a note of caution, but that is exactly what I am about to do. Why race a sailboat? Perhaps you have an answer ready: "To win, of course. You said so at the beginning, didn't you? And you have been trying to explain various ways of winning on every page. It would be pretty silly to say at this stage that it is not our purpose to win races."

All true. Yet I do say that this is not, after all, our *primary* purpose in racing sailboats. The real reason we race is that we enjoy it. "Oh, well, that's just begging the question: we enjoy it more when we finish up in the money." Very good. And just as long as that is indeed a fact, it *is* the reason for wanting to do better, and the reason for writing such a book as this and for reading it.

But there may come a time when you lose sight of this primary objective. It is entirely possible to become so involved in racing that winning becomes the end in itself, to the exclusion of everything else. You can get to the point where you don't see the woods for the trees in any highly competitive sport. You don't get very tensed up if you are finishing a race in last place, but you do if you are finishing a close first. It is a most unpleasant experience to be passed a hundred yards from the finish line. If winning the race becomes a matter of such grave importance to you that you begin developing ulcers on the way around the course, it is time to pause and take stock. Just why *are* you out there? Certainly not to make yourself miserable.

Perhaps this matter of tension is only an academic question

for anyone who does not customarily rate near the top of the score sheet. You may say, "Time enough to worry about worry when I get to be a champion. The situation doesn't arise back in the slums where I finish." May I suggest that you are too modest. You would not be reading this book if you were not on the way up in the yacht racing world; and you may find yourself in the winning column sooner than you think. It is true that doing well creates the problem I am talking about. It is much more relaxing to come from behind than to be required to defend a lead. To talk about an "unpleasant race" ought to be a contradiction in terms. All races should be fun. Yet the most unpleasant race I ever sailed was the last race of the 1954 North American Star championship at Rockport, Massachusetts. We went into that race with a four-point series lead, and had to watch it evaporate slowly, boat by boat, during the course of the afternoon as a fluky wind dropped us down to ninth place and moved the competitor we had been covering up to fifth so that he won series first on the resultant tie score.* The race would have been hardly any more enjoyable had we managed to finish eighth, although the series results would have been different. After that experience I did a lot of hard thinking about "the purpose of it all." Since then I have been racing as keenly as ever, and with as much spirit; but nowadays whenever things get up to fever pitch on the *Flame* I try to say to myself, "Relax, Jack; what do you think you are out here for anyway?" It helps one's perspective.

Harold S. Vanderbilt once wrote: "That windward leg against *Yankee* took more out of me than any other during the entire season, and I think we were all keenly disappointed. . . . When I got up the next morning, after a restless night, I felt that, if the other races affected me as this one had, I would not be able to stand the nervous strain of two weeks of continuous racing.

* I do an injustice to Jack Van Dyke in this one-sided account of a race which he sailed magnificently.

Something inside of me felt stretched; it seemed only a question of time when it might break." * And again: "I know of no better reducing diet than a closely-contested series of important match races." ** Vanderbilt was racing J-boats in America's Cup contests, a height to which most of us cannot hope to aspire. A great many other factors besides personal desires come into the picture when one becomes a public figure.*** But the fact remains that when racing turns into a nightmare, it is time to quit.

Let us ask another question: who is the most respected, the best remembered racing skipper? "The one who wins the most series, I guess." Then you guess wrong. People do *not* remember you for your trophies but for the way you sail, the quality of your sportsmanship. We again draw examples from America's Cup competition. What was the most memorable part of the 1934 cup races? Probably the unfortunate protest incidents and the acrimonious discussions stirred up by them. On the other hand, who is the best remembered British yachtsman? In the U.S. public mind it is certainly Sir Thomas Lipton, who never skippered any of his J-boats and never won the America's cup; but he was a noble sportsman.

Most youngsters have to race a few years before it dawns on them that a skipper makes a better record and in every way a more desirable and more memorable showing by withdrawing after a foul than by not doing so, even though by staying in the race he could have won the series (assuming he could get away

* Harold S. Vanderbilt, ENTERPRISE, (Scribner's, 1931) p. 116.

** Harold S. Vanderbilt, ON THE WIND'S HIGHWAY, (Scribner's, 1939) p. 25.

*** I was impressed by a remark made by Ted, the expert professional aboard de Coursey Fales' beautiful schooner *Nina,* on which I was privileged to sail an American Yacht Club cruise. These "cruises" consist of five days of port-to-port racing; and one day when we had done badly (which is not *Nina's* custom), Ted said glumly, "I don't care so much for ourselves"; (anyone could see that it was a real tragedy to him, though he wouldn't admit it); "but we have an obligation to our public: a lot of people have faith in *Nina.*" I doubt whether we small-boat skippers are entitled to such grandiose notions.

with the foul). Quite aside from the ethical aspect of the thing, series victories are at best temporal. Ask anyone to tell you who won last summer's such-and-such regatta, which seemed so important at the time, and he won't be able to remember; but if anybody's sportsmanship was a little off-color, he will remember who *that* was with no difficulty. The silver pot may be a nice prize; but it is by no means worth selling yourself short to get it. The skipper who has a reputation for leaning over backwards in his efforts to be fair is the one who is admired and honored above all others. It's practical, too, if you want to be hard-boiled about it: if you force yourself to withdraw from every dubious protest situation instead of attempting to brazen it out, you become increasingly cautious and as a result get into less and less trouble.

Like any hobby or sport worth doing, sailboat racing is an escape, not from reality but from some of its more humdrum aspects. Hardly anyone is completely his own boss on shore. Even the boss is responsible to someone or to some authority. On board your boat you are truly master of your destiny for a day. The only thing that can order you around is the weather; and somehow we take more kindly to the demands of the forces of nature than to those of our fellows. The sense of freedom from shore-going ties and worries, even though temporary, is a never failing source of refreshment to flagging spirits and balm to frayed nervous systems.

There is a deeply rooted but usually frustrated urge in all of us to excel in something. This is the drive behind all games: we not only enjoy *playing*; we want to *win*. In our business and professional lives most of us do well enough to get along; but it is the exceptional man who does really well, and becomes so good in his field that he can fairly lay claim to some degree of fame. The vast majority of people go through life without doing really well in anything. Here is a final motive behind small boat racing. It offers a chance to excel at something, at a cost within the reach of that national statistic, "the man of moderate means," and without the necessity of any special inborn talent or physical endowment. I believe this offer is one of the real and not unworthy reasons for the continuing popularity of the sport.

CHAPTER 15

Afterthought

The book was supposed to end with the last chapter; but the fact is that I have had such a good time writing it that I just don't like to stop. I hope you have enjoyed reading it half as much.

The only trouble with writing a book on anything is that it brands the author as an "expert" on the subject. I think that this is a deep conspiracy fostered by the people who write books. I do not feel in the least like an expert. Actually things are always in such a dither on the *Flame* that it is a perpetual surprise that we are able to win any races at all. (During one spell of bad races a couple of summers ago we got so out of the habit of arriving at the first mark first that when we finally did so we rounded it the wrong way!) No: in the last analysis, as we remarked at the end of the sail chapter, you must become your own expert. Writing a book serves to organize and crystallize one's thoughts. I think that I have learned more about my own racing methods by trying to explain them to you than you have by reading about them. So why not write one of your own? It doesn't have to be published. Start a log of your races right away. It's a lot of fun, it's a way to let off steam about the race, and it becomes a valuable source of review material from which to refresh your memory on how not to repeat old errors and how to re-exploit old discoveries. You have seen some samples from my logs. They contain also a record of hours on each sail, names of crews, details of trim, notations for possible improvements in hardware and so forth. It is all of value.

I leave you with a final admonition: think on these things.

Ponder. Cogitate. Dream. It is only by exercising the gray matter that you can improve your racing results. I am sure that this is true of any sport. But what makes yachting the *best* sport (naturally—could anyone question it?) is that thinking about it takes your mind not onto a cinder path, or a court, or a field; but onto a boat, which floats in blue water, under the summer sun, on the bay which you have come to love.

Index

abnormal means of checking way, 120
airport forecasts, 98
Allouette, 123
All Out of Step, Gerard B. Lambert, 83
American Yacht Club cruise, 139
America's Cup, 139
An Accomplishment of Sail, Ralph M. Monroe, 56
anemograph, 43
apparent wind, 14, 135
appendix, IYRU, 123
art of sailing, 2
Atlantic Monthly, 9

balance, hull, 131
barging, 36, 49
Barnegat Bay, 55
Barnes, Stanley, 36
barometer, 91
battens, Ch. 13; 73
Bavier, Robert N. Jr., 102
becalmed yacht, 121
boatyards, 6
booby-trap start, 50
Boomerang, 67
boom-jack, 130
Boston, 91
brain, human, 9
breaking in a sail, 126
Buzzards Bay, 43

Calahan, H. A., 43
calendering, 128
Canada, 92
cancelled race, 20, 40
centerboard, 132
center of effort, 131
center of lateral resistance, 131
Chapman, Charles F., 90
checking way, 120
Chesapeake Bay, 39
Chesapeake Bay Championship, 67
Chicago, 43
chronometer, race committee, 21
Circus, 55, 67
committee, race, Ch. 4, 11, 12; 17, 21, 25, 26, 30
Common Sense of Yacht Design, L. Francis Herreshoff, 134
cotton sails, Ch. 13
Council, RYA, Ch. 11, 12
course, shortening, 19
covering, 53, 60, 65
craftsmanship, 7
crew, Ch. 8; 4, 22, 106, 141
Cuba, 135
cumulus clouds, 100

dacron, Ch. 13
Day, Thomas Fleming, 89
Deacon, Arthur M., 26
Dickerson, Mahlon, 125
Dilke, Sir Fisher, 81
dinghies, 48, 78, 104, 125, 134
disallowing a race, 25, 40
Disaster at Dundee, John Prebble, 56
Dodd, Mead & Co., 83
Doubleday, 83
draft, 133
duck sails, Ch. 13
du Pont, E. I., 124
dust, 127

East Lepe, 81
Eaton's Point, 84
Egypt Point, 81
Enterprise, Harold S. Vanderbilt, 139
equipment, required, 106

Fales, de Coursey, 139
finish line, 60, 107, 120
Firth of Tay, 56

flaps, airplane wing, 131
Flower, 67
fog, 22, 24
forecasting weather, Ch. 10
fouling out, Ch. 11, 12; 11, 29, 68, 139
Franklin, Benjamin, 91
"freezing out" at start, 104
friction, surface of a sail, 126
fronts, weather, 90

gadgets, forecasting, 97
Gleam, 125
government marks, 83, 106
Great South Bay, L. I., 10
Gulf stream, 135
Gurnard Ledge, 81

hailing about, 115
Harcourt, Brace & Co., 43, 56
Hard Sails, Inc., 125
Harrison, George R., 9
Hazen, D. C., 131
header, tacking on, 44, 49, 54, 55
helm, 131
Herreshoff, L. Francis, 134
Hills, George E., 102
Houghton Mifflin, 127
Huntington Bay, 84
hurricanes, 91

ice boats, 56
intercollegiate racing, 48
interference from power boats, 60
International 110; 36, 77, 136
International Yacht Racing Union, Ch. 11, 12; 20, 39
isobars, 94

J-boats, 82, 139
Jenkins, Herbert, Ltd., 82
Jersey Coast Challenge, 55
jibsheets, 13
Just One Little Thing, C. T. Ludington, 127

Knapp, Arthur, 134

L-16, 136
Lake Erie, 43
Lake Michigan, 44, 69
Lambert, Gerard B., 82
Larchmont, N. Y., 62
lay line, 58, 62
leech of sail, 129
Lehnert, R. F., 131
Light on the Sailcloth Problem, Lingard and Paine, 128
Lightning, 36
Lingard, Thomas, 128
line squall, 99
Lippincott, Howard, 55
Lippincott, Robert, 125
Lipton, Sir Thomas, 139
log book, 17, 142
Long Island Sound, 84, 98
Loomis, Alfred F., 86
Ludington, C. T., 127

maintenance, 6, 80
map, weather, 94
mast, 16, 132
mast line, 114
McNulty series, 68
memory bank, 96
meteorology, Ch. 10
Mexico, 92
Miller Memorial series, 67
Milwaukee, Wis., 68
mind, human, 8
Mississippi Valley, 90
Monroe, Ralph M., 56
Mosbacher, Emil Jr., 80
Motor Boating, 90, 127
multi-mitred jib, 128
Murchie, Guy, 127

nap of sailcloth, 127
Naples, Italy, 38
New England, 93, 95
New Yacht Racing Rules, The, Robert N. Bavier, Jr., 102
New York City, 98
Nina, 139
normal course, 115
North American Championship, Star class, 24, 55, 125, 138
North American Yacht Racing Union, Ch. 11, 12; 18, 20, 39
northeaster, 93
northwester, Ch. 5; 54, 96, 102
Norton, W. W. & Co., 2, 102
Nye, Harry G. Jr., 38
nylon, 124

Observer on Ranger, Sir Fisher Dilke, 82
Olympic Games, 112
On and Off Soundings, 56
On the Wind's Highway, Harold S. Vanderbilt, 139
orlon, Ch. 13
overlap, 69, 104
overstanding, 34, 62, 67, 76
overtaking, 114

Paine, F. Ward, 128
Penguin, 39
Philadelphia, 91
Piloting, Seamanship and Small Boat Handling, Charles F. Chapman, 90
Pleasures of Sailing, The, Alfred Stanford, 9
plexiglass, 135
postponement, 19
power boats, interference from, 60
Prebble, John, 56
Proctor, Ian, 78
proper way, 115
Properties, NAYRU, 122

Race Your Boat Right, Arthur Knapp, 134
Racing Dinghy Handling, Ian Proctor, 78
radially cut jib, 130
radio, 98
rake, 132
reach, 22, 49, 76, 102
reçall, Ch. 4; 21, 68, 69, 118, 122
reefing, 5
re-sail, 26
rigging, 10, 132
Rockport, Mass., 138
room at marks, 104
Ross, Robert & Co., Ltd., 78
rounding the course, 118
Royal Yachting Association, 106
Rudder Publishing Co., 134
run, 22

safe leeward, 61
Sailing Rules in Yacht Racing, The, George E. Hills, 102
sails, Ch. 13; 2
sails, changing, 18
San Francisco Bay, 43
Scientific American, 131
Scientific Sailboat Racing, Ted Wells, 83
score, series, Ch. 7; 20
Scotch Mist, 67
Scribner's Sons, Chas., 102, 139
"secrets," 15
series score, Ch. 7; 20
shortening course, 19
Snipes, 136
Solent, 82
Song of the Sky, Guy Murchie, 127
spectator boats, 60
spinnakers, 74, 106
sportsmanship, 139
Stanford, Alfred, 9
Stars, 3, 16, 24, 26, 36, 69, 80, 112, 125, 136
station bills, 73
Stearns, Richard I., 68
stopwatch, 21
submarine, 22
Successful Yacht Racing, C. S. Ogilvy, 2, 44, 123
surface friction, sailcloth, 126
synthetics, Ch. 13; 2

tacking ship, 12
tactics, 20
tactics, starting, Ch. 4
Tay bridge, 56
tension, mental, 137
thunderstorm, 5, 39, 96, 99
tide, Ch. 9; 68, 76
time limit, 20
timing starts, 73
Toronto, Canada, 24
Torrey, Owen C. Jr., 134
"tower clouds," 100
Trevor, J. B., 43
trim, 46, 54, 65, 141
turbulence, 55, 127

underwater part of a mark, 120
unsafe leeward, 61
U.S. Navy, 22

Vanderbilt, Harold S., 138
Van Dyke, Jack, 138
vang, 130
Van Nostrand & Co., D., 56, 134
Vega, 67

vote of skippers, 26

wake, 60
weather helm, 131
Webb, Jack, 36
Wells, Ted A., 83
White Shadow, 67
Wind and Tide in Yacht Racing, Calahan and Trevor, 43
window in sail, 135

Yachting, 86, 112, 128
Yankee, 138
yards, 6